"WAY to go!"

Tales and Tips
To
Help You Along The Path To Heaven

PETER J. MORIARTY

"WAY to go!"

ISBN-13:978-1977572059

ISBN-10:1977573057

Dedication

To my wife, Elizabeth, and our children, Paul, Kerry, and Richard, who have contributed so much to the joy of my life and for whom I am eternally grateful to God.

To the priests of St. Patrick's Catholic Community and the friars of The Franciscan Renewal Center, Scottsdale, who have guided and nourished my Christian beliefs and development over many years.

And last, and certainly not least, to my deceased parents, Ann and Bill Moriarty, who taught me so much and with so much love. In particular, I would also like to acknowledge the following impactful words spoken to me by my father when I was a teenager:

"Every day that I live, I am one day closer to my death."

Preface

I was fortunate to have a very happy childhood. I was not an easy child. "Boisterous" was probably the kindest way to describe me, but I was fortunate enough to have loving parents and sisters who taught me both by example and by setting boundaries as to what I could and could not do. Later, as a teenager at boarding school in England, I learned the lessons of how to behave in society. I learned, sometimes the hard way, about acting responsibly and with true self-discipline. I certainly feel that I benefited greatly, both from my happy home life and from the educational and athletic opportunities that boarding school provided for me. I emerged in my late teens and early twenties as an ambitious, goal-oriented individual. "Determined" was probably then the kindest way to describe me at that point in time. I was certainly ambitious, and it was clearly that characteristic that resulted in me and my young family leaving our home country of Great Britain to live in a number of different counties for quite a few years before settling here in the United States. I was determined to gain significant management experience at a comparatively young age. Subsequently, it was again my blind ambition and determination that drove me to start a number of companies, a couple of which were very successful and others that lost me and, more importantly, our investors, significant amounts of money.

This was all in pursuit of my worldly goals. Why did I do it? Why was I so totally committed to achieving those goals? Why was I so ambitious for material success? In more recent years, I have tried to explore those questions as a means to obtaining a better understanding of myself and what I need to do to successfully pursue my spiritual goal: to ensure that I am traveling on the right path to safely get me to Heaven. I have tried to get to grips with identifying what were the driving forces in my worldly ambitions. I have also attempted to discern what lessons I can draw on to help me successfully travel along my spiritual path, and it is the telling of these tales and tips that constitute the content of this book. My sincere hope is that each chapter might provide you with points to ponder and reflect upon as you travel along your own personal path to Heaven. I hope that you will hear those internal voices of encouragement shouting out to you, "Way to go!" Remember that "Christ is the Way" as well as being "the Truth and the Life" and that after his death, Christ's disciples were known as followers of the "WAY." We, too, are his disciples. "WAY to go!"

"WAY to go!"

Peter J. Moriarty

1 John 4:11-12

Beloved, if God so loved us, we also must love one another. No one has ever seen God. Yet if we love one another, God remains in us, and His love is brought to perfection in us.

Chapter

1

I was an extremely boisterous child. "Boisterous" is probably a kind word. I was mischievous and not always very good at following the rules. Just as an example, at the age of four, having been sent to my bedroom for being naughty, I, apparently, opened my bedroom window, which was on the second floor, and then proceeded to climb out and slide down the drainpipe. I then knocked on the front door, much to the surprise of my parents.

I had to be disciplined because I clearly could not discipline myself. I knew that my parents loved me, but I needed to be told firmly what the parameters were in which I could operate. I, all too often, had to be reprimanded for doing something wrong. I just didn't seem to learn. On occasions, I did, of course, have to be punished, and that fear of punishment helped remind me that my mom and dad were being serious about my need to behave.

I needed to know and understand what I could and could not do. I needed to appreciate the parameters beyond which I could not go without risking their displeasure and the possibility of punishment.

It was my parents' love for me that made them put the effort into caring about the way I behaved. It must have been hard work for them because I was a real "handful." They could have just as easily let me have my own (selfish) way, and I would surely have grown up a self-centered, badly adjusted, socially irresponsible individual. If they had not taken the trouble or made the effort to correct me, they would not have been very loving parents.

As I got older and matured, I started to exert self-control, and I behaved out of love and respect for my parents, my family, and the other people around me.

That is not dissimilar to the developmental path that many of us experience as Christians. We start by thinking of God in terms of the One who punishes us for breaking the rules, for sinning. As we mature, we come to the realization and appreciation that God loves us—that God is love and that love is unselfish. Love does not put itself first. Love suffers for the sake of others.

As a loving parent, God wants us to learn the importance of love. God wants us to learn that love is manifested in the way we treat one another: the way we treat our fellow man. That is why He, in the form of Jesus Christ, came onto this earth to teach us and to lead us to love one another.

We, however, are born intrinsically selfish. Sociologists tell us that most children until the age of seven believe that the world revolves around them. It is the parents who teach the child, by word, and particularly by example, the difference between right and wrong—between selfish and unselfish acts. Children need to know what is right and what is wrong.

To guide us through our childhood, we learn that transgressions are called sins. They are deeds or actions or thoughts that are intrinsically self-centered. If you think about it, sins are really about "putting me first." They are opposed to the standard of love that God, as our parent, wants us to display.

As we mature in our knowledge of God and in our Christian beliefs, we move away from the concept of sin, fear, and punishment to an understanding of doing things that will keep us in a loving relationship with God.

As we mature, we, hopefully, stop doing so many things wrong, not because of fear of punishment but because we realize that they are selfish. We try to exert self-control— to behave in the manner our loving heavenly parent, God, wants us to behave: loving others, putting others before ourselves, and being concerned for, and showing mercy towards, the less fortunate in our society.

That is the central message that Christ tried to communicate to us during his life on earth: God is love, and as stated in 1 John 4:18:

"There is no fear in love,
but perfect love drives out fear
because fear has to do with punishment,
and so one who fears is not yet perfect in love."

Therefore, the child is not yet perfect in love, but the mature Christian (hopefully you and I) should be a person who focuses on loving, not fearing, God and loving our fellow man.

As St. John also wrote in his first letter (4:11-13), "Beloved, if God so loved us, we also must love one another."

That is the difference between the Christian who has not matured past the "sin, punishment, and fear" stage in their life and the Christian who has come to appreciate that if we truly love God, we will want to avoid doing things that we know are wrong, that we know are selfish, and that we know will impede our relationship with God and our fellow man.

Remember, "if God so loved us, we also must love one another." Hard as it may seem, this means that we sometimes have to be very careful about what we think, say, and do to other people, and it also means than we have to love even those who in our eyes might seem "unlovable."

Travel Tip to Remember
God accepts us for who we are. He loves us unconditionally, no matter who we are or what we have done in the past. For our part, we must put in the effort to drive out our intrinsic selfishness so that we can, in turn, love God and our fellow man unconditionally.

"WAY to go!"

Matthew 8: 2 - 3

And then a leper approached, did him homage, and said, "Lord, if you wish, you can make me clean." He stretched out his hand, touched him, and said, "I will do it. Be made clean." His leprosy was cleansed immediately.

Chapter

2

I grew up learning the typical prayers of a Catholic. The "Our Father, Hail Mary, Glory be to the Father," etc. They were just words that I said. As I got a little older, I would participate with the rest of the family in saying the rosary. My mother and father would get down on their knees in the living room and we, the children, were expected to do the same. We would say the rosary together as a family.

I would say the words, and keep on and on, probably thinking to myself, "When is this going to end?" At that age, they were probably just words to me…almost a meaningless chant.

However, I was always impressed by the love that my mother and father had for the practice of our faith and their attention to daily prayer. I, therefore, thought that it must be a good thing even if I considered it somewhat boring at that age.

The reality was that, for many years, I didn't know what half the words meant. Just as an example, my mom, dad, and sisters would always kiss me before I went to bed (I was the youngest), and we would each say to the other "G'night G'bless." It was only years later that I found out that what I was meant to be saying was, in fact, "Good night. God bless." "G'night G'bless" was just another example of me saying words without really knowing what I was saying: a meaningless chant.

Unfortunately, old habits die hard, and many of us still probably feel that we have to continually repeat prayers the way we were taught as children instead of speaking to God as a real person. I certainly had to make real efforts to free myself of this habit of repeatedly and thoughtlessly saying words instead of prayers. I had to learn to be open and honest with God: to have God as a real person in my life.

This was an important development for me because some time ago I had started to wonder if I really did love God; I didn't seem to feel the same way about God as I do about my wife and children.

I wanted to love God with my whole heart and my whole soul and my whole being, but in order to do so, I really had to try to relate to him better. Therefore, I decided to tell him exactly that: that I felt as though I didn't really love Him and that I wanted to and that I needed His help.

I know that God heard my prayers and continues to help me. I am not chanting meaningless words so much anymore.

In the New Testament, we see an example of the exact opposite of meaningless chant as prayers. We hear an almost perfect prayer coming from someone who has fallen off the edges of society—an outcast who was not even allowed to participate in the Jewish religion because he was not allowed in the community as he was considered "unclean" due to his disease of leprosy.

Nevertheless, despite this marginalization, the leper truly knew how to pray. He knew how to ask the Son of God for what he, the leper, truly desired. He said it perfectly—and perfectly unselfishly. "Lord, if you wish, you can make me clean." And we then read that Jesus was moved with pity and said to the leper, "I will do it. Be made clean."

The leper used words or an approach that is not all that different to the words that Jesus used in the Garden of Gethsemane, namely, "Father, everything is possible for you. Take this cup from me. Yet not what I will, but what you will."

If each of us could only pray in the same way, we would be treating God as a real person with whom we have a real relationship. We would be showing our love for, and our trust in, God, telling Him that we accept whatever is His will. We would be selflessly placing ourselves in His hands.

That is the type of prayer to which we should all aspire but appreciate that we might frequently fall short unless we continually treat God like a real person and ask Him for his continued help.

Travel Tip to Remember
Talk to God as you would to a close member of your family for whom you have tremendous love and respect: someone whom you trust to always do the right thing for you and whose advice and guidance you willingly follow.

Peter J. Moriarty

Luke 11:1-2

One day Jesus was praying in a certain place. When he finished, one of his disciples said to him, "Lord, teach us to pray, just as John taught his disciples. He said to them, "When you pray, say:
Father, hallowed be your name, your Kingdom come..."

Chapter

3

When I was about seven years of age, I had a best friend who was also called Peter. He was about a year older than me and always had cool toys and, apparently, the latest and greatest of everything.

I remember that Peter appeared one day in a Davy Crocket, coon-skin hat his dad had bought him. The Davy Crocket movie had just been released in England, and it was enormously popular among all my friends. I really wanted a Davy Crocket hat just like my friend Peter, so I asked my Dad if he would buy one for me. I pleaded with him, but he still said no. However, he also took the opportunity to add a few words of explanation: "It's 'No,' Peter, because you have to learn that you can't have everything that you want in life."

As I got older, and certainly when I became a parent myself, I realized just how wise and loving my father was. He was quite strict. He communicated the rules and set the boundaries of what I could do and what I could not do. But I also knew that he would always do his best for me. He would try to give me what I asked for, provided it was in my best interests. He also gave me a terrific example by the way he led his life: by the things he said and the things he did.

As an adult, I have matured into having a clear appreciation of what the rules and boundaries are in my life. I have learned what I can and cannot do. My focus now is on trying to lead the type of life and be the type of person of whom my father would have been truly proud.

Isn't that the way, you and I should think about our Heavenly Father? We need to focus on being the type of person our Heavenly Father is truly proud of, but in order to achieve this, we first need to make every effort to make sure that we know the Father and what He has taught us and imparted to us through the teachings and example of His son, Jesus. As we mature as Christians, we have to try to better understand the Father and what it is that He has been trying to teach us so far throughout our lives.

For many of us, I suspect that we have spent most of our early lives thinking of God as this bearded old man in the sky: an image of God as someone who is easily displeased with us if we do things wrong—a God who is out to catch us and condemn us to hellfire for "breaking his laws."

This is so far from the truth. This is a negative and misleading image of God. After all, we have to remember that it was Jesus himself who taught us to call God, "Our Father." Jesus said that we should use the name "Abba" when praying to God. "Abba" in Aramaic means "Dear Father" or, as some would translate it, "Daddy." It is a very intimate and trusting word. This is quite incredible. Jesus tells us that we should call our Creator, the Lord of all things, "Dear Father" or "Daddy." That means that we are truly sons and daughters of God—God is our heritage.

Essentially, we have spiritual DNA in us, and we can be absolutely confident that our Father always has our best interests at heart, even more so than our earthly fathers.

We are truly sons and daughters of God. The trouble is that most of us don't believe this or have trouble thinking of God, our Father, in that way. But we are.

When we start to clearly think and deeply believe that God is truly our Father, then we take a completely different approach to leading our lives. Our whole relationship with God takes on a very different light. We are not so concerned about avoiding wrong. We are more concerned about doing right: doing what is good. We are more concerned about being the sons and daughters of whom the Father is truly proud. We can feel confident in our Father's generosity and love for us, appreciating that he will grant us whatever we ask for, provided it is good for us. Not giving a child everything they ask for is often a pure act of love and concern for that child's future development and well-being…even if it is a Davy Crocket hat.

Travel Tip to Remember
Wholeheartedly accept that you can't have everything that you want in life. Stop chasing after things and, particularly, material possessions. Ask God for what you need, but fully appreciate that a loving father will only give his child what he believes to be in the best interests of the child. Why would God, our Father, do anything differently? He has our best interests at heart.

Peter J. Moriarty

John 3:16-17

For God so loved the world that he gave his one and only Son, that whoever believes in him shall not perish but have eternal life. For God did not send his Son into the world to condemn the world, but to save the world through him.

Chapter

4

My life has been very much influenced by my father. I think that in many ways, I hero-worshiped him because he was a very righteous man. He stood up for what he believed in. I learned early on in life that he was a man of absolute moral integrity in business and in his personal life, and he loved my mother dearly, which was absolutely evident from the things he said to her and the way he treated her. For her part, my mother was everything that a child could want. She was loving, caring, and fun. She was always the life and soul of the party. But as a male, I naturally looked to my father as my hero, and he has been my guiding light throughout my adult life, even though he died many years ago.

I believed in my father. So the question is: what does that mean?

For me it means that I looked up to him and wanted, and still want, to do the things he would be proud of. I did not, and do not, want to let him down.

We read the words in St. John's gospel, "So that everyone who believes in him (Jesus) may have eternal life."

So what does that mean "everyone who believes in him may have eternal life?" Does it mean that just because you believe that Jesus really existed that you may have eternal life?

I presume that most of us would immediately say that we believe that Jesus existed, but can we say that we believe in Jesus in the same way that I described with my father. "I looked up to him and wanted, and still want, to do the things he would be proud of. I did not, and do not, want to let him down."

I think that that is really the essence of believing in Jesus: a positive desire to conduct our lives in such a way that we can feel confident that Jesus will be proud of us. It is not about avoiding sin. It is about actively doing good, just as Jesus taught us to.

However, in order to get to that point, I think that we have to make every effort to know and experience Jesus in our lives. Can we do that? Have we experienced Jesus as a living person?

No. Certainly not in the same way as the apostles. So it is tough. I think that we get to know Jesus not just by reading the New Testament but by thinking deeply, praying intensely, and making every effort to fully consider and ultimately understand what Jesus was trying to communicate to us. When we do this, we mature as Christians, and we are ultimately left with a determination to live lives of which Jesus would be proud. We mature just as I matured in the understanding of what my earthly father had been trying to teach me in my early life.

Travel Tip to Remember
Develop a positive desire to conduct your life in such a way that you can actually feel confident that Jesus will be

proud of you. Focus on doing good instead of just focusing on avoiding sin.

1 Samuel 17:48-50

The Philistine then moved to meet David at close quarters, while David ran quickly toward the battle line to meet the Philistine. David put his hand into the bag and took out a stone, hurled it with the sling, and struck the Philistine on the forehead. The stone embedded itself in his brow, and he fell on his face to the ground. Thus David triumphed over the Philistine with sling and stone; he struck the Philistine dead, and did it without a sword in his hand.

Matthew 14:6-11

But at a birthday celebration for Herod, the daughter of Herodias performed a dance before the guests and delighted Herod so much that he swore to give her whatever she might ask for. Prompted by her mother, she said, "Give me here on a platter the head of John the Baptist." The king was distressed, but because of his oaths and the guests who were present, he ordered that it be given, and he had John beheaded in the prison. His head was brought in on a platter and given to the girl, who took it to her mother.

Chapter

5

From the age of 11 through 18, I attended a boarding
school in the north of England. It was a particularly cold
and damp place. It had a lot of wind and rain and could
really be quite bleak. Every Monday afternoon, in the
winter months, we would have to go on a cross-country
run, irrespective of the weather. Frequently, the route took
us through what was referred to as "Mud Farm" or "Muck
Farm." It was aptly named; throughout most of the year,
you were running through ankle to knee-high mud—and
the farmyard excrement that was mixed in with it.

Some of my friends would try to avoid Mud Farm.
Sometimes, they would cheat and take a different route.
Sometimes they would try to talk me into going with them,
but as far as I recall, I always went through Mud Farm.
However, I could never figure out why the school insisted
that we go cross-country running—and why we had to run
such a miserable route. The only thing I did know for
certain was that once I got through Mud Farm, I would
arrive at the top of a hill and could cruise all the way down
the hill to the finishing line back at the school. In essence,
things always got better after Mud Farm.

Years later, I started to realize and appreciate why the
school considered cross country runs with miserable routes
as an essential part of life. As I went through business and
spiritual challenges, I started to appreciate that it was
frequently very similar to trying to run through mud and
muck in the rain, with a freezing cold wind. It took a lot of

effort and true perseverance to make it to the finishing line. It taught me that if I could make it through the difficult times—if I could approach those difficult times with determination to get through them, trusting that God had a plan for me—then things would work out. I needed to trust but also be prepared for whatever was thrown at me on the way.

I also began to appreciate the value of not giving in to peer pressure to take a short cut, even though it may have relieved me from running through Mud Farm. If I had done so, I would probably never have learned the lesson or the value of accepting and dealing with hard times and trusting in God. This was a very valuable lesson, both materially and spiritually. In both the Old and the New Testaments, we gain an appreciation for the value of being able to accept hard times…when perseverance, determination, and trust in God are absolutely necessary.

In the Old Testament, we hear of the success of David when, against all odds, he beat the giant, Goliath. He did not run away from the challenge that God put before him. He carried on regardless. He trusted in God, and he beat the giant and led his people to victory. Would you have bet on David?

In the New Testament, we hear of King Herod not having the courage of his convictions when the daughter of Salome said she wanted the head of John the Baptist. Herod caved in. He succumbed to peer pressure even though he was the king. He knew it was a totally unreasonable request to behead John the Baptist, but nevertheless he agreed to it.

That particular reading caused me to ask myself, "How often have I not spoken up for what I believe in? How often have I gone along with the crowd? In meetings, both formal and informal, how often have I kept quiet when I disagreed with things that others were saying just because I did not want to be unpopular or because I did not want to 'rock the boat'?"

During my time in boarding school, I would also worry a lot about the school subjects that I was not good at. I would spend a tremendous amount of time trying to revise those subjects. However, as I matured, I began to realize that the key to success was to identify my strengths (and we all have strengths) and focus on strengthening my strengths. My goal then became to be the very best that I could be at what I was already good at...instead of focusing on my weaknesses.

In the Old Testament story of David and Goliath, we have a great example of this. Little David is pitched against the mighty giant, Goliath, an experienced warrior with the body of the Incredible Hulk and a well-made spear and shield. What chance did David have? He was no match for Goliath. He lacked the build or physical stature of Goliath. He lacked the experience and fighting instruments. David did, however, trust in God, and he knew his strengths. He knew that he was very good with the slingshot. That was one of his definite strengths, and he was clearly the very best he could be at it. So, with a tiny slingshot, little David beat the giant, Goliath.

This is a great lesson for us all. We all know our own weaknesses, but we should also be very aware of our strengths. We need to ask ourselves, "Do I recognize the gifts that I have?" I am often amazed at how little some people think of themselves when I can see such great ability and inner beauty in them. None of us think that we are good enough to be saints. Nevertheless, we all have intrinsic qualities that are unique.

Do you know your own qualities? Do you know your own strengths?

We should each identify them and focus on strengthening those strengths to be the very best that we can be; then we will be even more assured of victory.

Travel Tip to Remember
Take time to consider your particular qualities and appreciate your inner beauty. Recognize the gifts you have. Focus on what you are already good at instead of focusing on your weaknesses. Accept that there are going to be hard times, but be determined not to give in to self-pity or peer pressure. Always do the right thing, no matter the consequences, knowing that by trusting in God you will gain the strength and courage to overcome all obstacles.

"WAY to go!"

Peter J. Moriarty

Philippians 2:3

Do nothing out of selfishness or out of vainglory; rather, humbly regard others as more important than yourselves.

Chapter

6

When I was at boarding school I was quite a gifted athlete. I represented our school at the 100 and 200 meter sprints. However, I never once represented the school in the 400 meter event. I liked the 100 and 200 meter events but intensely disliked the 400 meter race.

Nevertheless, at the end of each athletic season, on our school's annual athletics day, I always won the 400 meter finals. I did this by making sure that I got through the heats and just scraped my way into the finals. Then at the start of the final, I would make sure that I got behind the leader, staying in second or third position for the first part of the race. I would tuck myself in and let someone else face the resistance of the wind, at least for that first half of the race. I was saving myself so that when I reached the halfway mark, with only 200 meters left to run, I would tell myself that this was now the beginning of a 200 meter race, and I was going to win it…and I always did. I won that race just once every year, and that was in the finals of the annual athletics day event.

As I got older and began to reflect on how I could become a better Christian and the areas where I needed to improve, I started to think about my attitude towards the 400 meter race. I asked myself why I did that. It seems to me that I was out to prove not just that I had a God-given gift as an athlete but, perhaps more particularly, I was out to show other people that I was a better athlete than they were— that I was the "top dog." I obviously wanted to show that I could win when I wanted to—that while one or two other athletes might represent the school in the 400 meter race throughout the season, I could always win the race in the end.

Looking back now, I see that there was something intrinsically wrong about that. That was the sin of Pride. I was not content to accept that God had given me a gift for which I should be grateful. I needed to feed my ego by attempting to show that I was better than other people.

I am sure that this is something that many of us battle with each day: the need to prove that we are better than others. Why is it that we human beings act in this way? There is nothing wrong with someone acknowledging that they are intelligent, smart, gifted, good looking, wealthy, or whatever. The trouble is that most of us are not content with that. We want to be more intelligent than, smarter than, more gifted than, better looking than, or wealthier than someone else.

Because of this failing, the person who has the sin of Pride would be very unhappy if they thought everyone was just as intelligent, just as smart, just as gifted, just as good looking, or just as wealthy as they were. A real manifestation of the sin of pride is where, in order for us to feel good about ourselves or a particular situation, we have to feel that someone else is not as good as we are.

In his book, *Mere Christianity*, C. S. Lewis points out that this self-centered sin of Pride is one of the biggest problems, if not the biggest, that the human race has to face. We are taught that it was Pride that turned the Arc

Angel Lucifer against God. We have to turn ourselves away from always needing to prove that we are better than someone else. This drags us down. It can cause greed, corruption, and self-satisfied arrogance.

After years of thinking that I was merely "competitive," I now realize that many of my earlier actions and activities were driven by my desire to prove that I was better than others. This is definitely the darker side of ego: It is pride. It becomes a vice, and I believe that it is a vice that affects many of us. Furthermore, I think it is important that we recognize that while we have to be determined to turn away from this tendency to commit the sin of Pride, it is only by God's help, God's grace, that we can be free of it forever.

Travel Tip to Remember
There is a distinct difference between being competitive and being determined to show someone else that they are not as good as you are. There is a fine line between being grateful to God for your gifts or talents and wanting to rub someone else's face in it. In travelling along the path to Heaven, it is important to avoid the sin of Pride or self-centered arrogance.

Peter J. Moriarty

2 Timothy 4:7

I have competed well; I have finished the race; I have kept the faith.

Luke 1:37

... for nothing will be impossible for God.

Chapter

7

When I was at school, I hated training at the beginning of the season, irrespective of the sport. I went through mental and physical agony, as I had to get my body into top shape. I knew the level of pain that I had to go through. I knew what I had to do, but I would keep putting it off.

Our coaches would push me. They would keep telling me what I had to do. I would keep thinking to myself that it was alright for them—all they had to do was tell me what to do. I was the one going through the pain. They were not. They didn't provide me with the strength or energy that I needed to push myself to the limits.

I was thinking about this recently, and it happened at a time when I had also been thinking quite deeply about my religious beliefs and my life on earth. This included the normal questions that many people ask, such as, "Why am I here? What was God's reason for creating mankind? What is going to happen to me when I die?" These are the conclusions at which I arrived:

First, that God intended us all to achieve eternal life.

Second, since God's plan was always to come among us in the form of Jesus Christ so as to bring about our salvation, I have no choice but to firmly believe that by his teachings and by his example, Jesus was clearly showing us how to behave if we are to be members of the Kingdom of Heaven.

Third, that in following Jesus, we have to fully appreciate that his teaching was not focused on the negatives, such as "don't do this" and "don't do that." His teachings were focused on doing the positives in life. It was about loving and taking care of your neighbor: putting others before yourself.

I also came to the conclusion that once we have passed from this earthly existence, the Kingdom of Heaven is one where God's followers, through God's grace, have been purged of their egos and their intrinsic selfishness. They are selfless creatures embodied into the pure, unconditional love of their Creator: God. By abandoning all selfishness, they have enabled all of the intrinsic goodness, or should I say "Godness," inside of them to show itself. They are beings who have conquered their natural instinct for self-preservation and self-serving—beings who love God and God's creations rather than satisfying their own selfish desires.

Finally, I concluded that I, and in fact none of us, should leave it to the last minute of our lives on earth to get fit for eternal life. I concluded that we all need to start training now—no matter how painful it is—no matter what the sacrifice. We have to be fit for Heaven.

I may have hated training at school, but now, in my adult life, I am faced with the far more important task of preparing for eternal life. We all face the challenge of getting fit: the challenge of training to be a creature fit for the Kingdom of Heaven. We can't keep putting it off, as I tried to do with my sports training.

Each of us needs to be open to God: to trust in God. Just as God raised up his only son, Jesus, God can do great things for each and every one of us. Nothing is impossible for God. Therefore, no matter how challenging the situation might appear to be, it is never too early to start training: training to be fit for eternal life. It's not impossible if we ask God to be our trainer, and trust in His teachings, guidance, and advice.

Travel Tip to Remember
If you truly want to prepare for a successful journey to Heaven, take positive action to perfect selflessness. Trust in God. Put your ego aside and always be considerate of others before yourself.

Peter J. Moriarty

Mark 10:17-22

As he was setting out on a journey, a man ran up, knelt down before him, and asked him, "Good teacher, what must I do to inherit eternal life?" Jesus answered him, "Why do you call me good? No one is good but God alone. You know the commandments: 'You shall not kill; you shall not commit adultery; you shall not steal; you shall not bear false witness; you shall not defraud; honor your father and your mother.'" He replied and said to him, "Teacher, all of these I have observed from my youth." Jesus, looking at him, loved him and said to him, "You are lacking in one thing. Go, sell what you have, and give to [the] poor and you will have treasure in heaven; then come, follow me." At that statement his face fell, and he went away sad, for he had many possessions.

Chapter

8

When I was at school, I loved playing rugby. It was all-consuming for me. In fact, I had a recurring dream about rugby. In my dream, I would always get past my opponents, no matter how big they were, and I would always score a touchdown (referred to as a "try" in rugby). Nothing could stop me in my dream. The truth is, I played on the first team, which is the equivalent of the varsity team, from age 14 until I graduated school at 18, and I did score a touchdown in a great many of those games.

My brain seemed to visualize the future. It was as though I knew the outcome or, at least, I had subconsciously convinced myself that I knew the outcome. I was going to get past the opponent. My brain had become wired with the conviction that I was going to score the touchdown. Nothing and no one was going to stop me, no matter what the pain. I knew what I wanted. I was totally convinced.

I try to apply the same principles to my work today. I am big on setting written goals. I like to start with visualizing the future: identifying what it is that I want to achieve and then working backwards, defining each step that needs to be taken in order to achieve the goal.

This becomes my priority. Essentially, my brain filters out everything that is not going to help me achieve my goal. I, therefore, don't become distracted by other "perceived" priorities.

This may be the way many of us operate in business, but what about in our spiritual lives?

Do you have a set of spiritual goals?

Surely, our number one goal in life has to be to inherit eternal life. That is certainly what God intends for us. In the New Testament, we read of Jesus saying to the 72 disciples, "Rejoice because your names are written in Heaven."

So what should we each be doing to be sure that we inherit eternal life?

Well we first have to be sure that that is what we really want—that that is the priority on which our brain focuses. We may say it, we may verbalize it, but are we really thinking about it? Is our brain convinced that that is our first priority?

For my part I know that I need to think about it constantly, to dream about it just as I did with rugby. It has to be my priority—my major goal. Its achievement must be what drives my whole being.

If we are serious about inheriting eternal life, then we should write that down as a goal. Once the goal has been defined in writing, then we should work backwards. We should put in writing what the key things are that we need to do through the rest of our lives in order to inherit eternal life.

Travel Tip to Remember

Visualize your future as having achieved your goal of eternal life. Implant that goal in your brain. Let your brain filter out everything and anything that will not assist you in achieving that goal and particularly those things that will prevent you from achieving it. Know what you want and go after it with your whole heart, your whole mind, and your whole soul. Be determined that nothing and nobody is going to stop you from "going over that touch-line" and winning your place in Heaven.

Peter J. Moriarty

Acts 2:43-47

Awe came upon everyone, and many wonders and signs were done through the apostles. All who believed were together and had all things in common; they would sell their property and possessions and divide them among all according to each one's need. Every day they devoted themselves to meeting together in the temple area and to breaking bread in their homes. They ate their meals with exultation and sincerity of heart, praising God and enjoying favor with all the people. And every day the Lord added to their number those who were being saved.

Chapter

9

Many years ago, when I was in my mid-20s and living in England, my company sent me on my first business trip to Africa. I was very excited about the trip. On top of my excitement, I was also really pleased that my company was paying for me to fly first class, which I had never done before.

Well, the day arrived for my trip to West Africa. The company driver picked me up at my home early in the morning to drive me to Heathrow Airport in London. I had decided that, as I was flying first class, I should dress in what I considered to be the appropriate attire. So there I was in my best pinstriped suit, white shirt and appropriately conservative tie.

The flight took me from London to Amsterdam, Holland, and then from Amsterdam to Freetown, the capital of Sierra Leone.

On arriving in Sierra Leone it was almost as though I had a target painted on my back. There I was, a young man in a white shirt, conservative tie and a black pinstriped suit. I stepped off the plane into the heat of the African sun, clearly not realizing how out of place I looked. Then, all of a sudden, as I collected my luggage, I was descended upon. The locals seemed to swarm around me. I was offered every deal available. Many of them wanted to carry my bags (where to, I don't know), while others offered to be my guide and, in fact, provide anything I wanted.

They really could see me coming. I advertised it. They knew that this was a young man who didn't know what he was doing. This was someone who had clearly never been to Sierra Leone before—in fact, he had probably never been on the continent of Africa before. I looked like a rookie and probably the proverbial sucker.

What had I gotten myself into? Why did I travel in that black pinstriped suit?

I traveled in that suit because I thought that that was how people in first class traveled. That's what I knew as a child. First-class passengers were well dressed. Now, the reality was that I had failed to adapt to the particular circumstances of the "here and now." In particular, I had failed to think out where I was going.

As I recently reflected on this incident, I started to wonder how many of the things that I do in my life today are also incorrectly conditioned by the things that I learned as a child: the things that I presumed to be the right or appropriate things to do. I certainly know that, like so many people, I am very much a creature of habit.

I also started to wonder about how much of my life as a practicing Christian is merely a set of automatic responses or activities—responses or activities done without much thought as to why I do them rather than doing them because of my love for God and his son, Jesus Christ. I started to wonder if I had not really matured as a Christian.

I wondered if I was stuck in my childhood or adolescent perception of what being a Christian was all about.

I started to ask myself how many of the things that I do are, in reality, out of place for a mature Christian. Just for example, it might be stupid, but I feel a sense of guilt if I forget to say my morning or night prayers, while on the other hand, I don't seem to feel bad if I garble or rush my prayers without even realizing what I am saying. It's as though I am just repeating words as in my childhood, almost like a magic spell.

Do you ever feel like that?

As a result of my reflection, I concluded that I would like to spend time weeding out the bad habits and immature activities that seem to be so much a part of my Christian life. I decided that I would like to try to substitute them with attitudes and activities that are more reflective of a mature, committed Christian.

Once I had this change of attitude, I started to try to live my life as someone who is really conscious of and happy about the fact that Jesus came on this earth to show us how to lead our lives: a person who appreciates that Jesus came so that we may all have salvation. I now want to be someone who is not just a Christian on paper—I don't want to be someone who says his prayers or goes to church without thinking about what he is saying or doing. I don't want to be a Christian who has never grown up, who is only at the same level of maturity or development as he was in elementary or even high school. I want to progress way beyond that. I want to be an educated adult Christian.

I want to progress to being a true believer in Jesus Christ: the type of Christian that we hear about in the early life of the church—a Christian who is full of joy, conviction, and commitment because of what Jesus did for him and what Jesus has taught him to do in the way he leads his life. That is why Jesus was born. That is why Jesus died for us. That is why Jesus rose for us.

How about you? Where are you in your development as a Christian?

Travel Tip to Remember
Don't be stuck in the past. Go beyond elementary or high school Christianity. Have the guts to practice Christianity the way you know it should be lived...as an adult. Bring yourself up to date. Educate yourself and act as a mature Christian. Lead your Christian life with commitment, determination, and most of all with joy in the knowledge that Jesus showed us how to live our lives, and by His dying and rising showed us the promise of eternal life. Enjoy your Christianity.

"WAY to go!"

Peter J. Moriarty

Matthew 4:18-22

*As he was walking by the Sea of Galilee, he saw two
brothers, Simon who is called Peter, and his brother
Andrew, casting a net into the sea; they were fishermen.
He said to them, "Come after me, and I will make you
fishers of men." At once they left their nets and followed
him. He walked along from there and saw two other
brothers, James, the son of Zebedee, and his brother John.
They were in a boat, with their father Zebedee, mending
their nets. He called them, and immediately they left their
boat and their father and followed him.*

Chapter

10

Do you ever look back on events in your life and wonder to yourself, "Why did I ever do that?" "What drove me to take that action?" "Why did I ever make that decision?" "What was the driving force behind that move?" "How did my actions affect those I love?"

Well, I certainly have. I know that many of the decisions I made in my twenties and thirties were the result of overwhelming ambition and blind determination.

Let me first give you a bit of background to my life during my twenties and thirties.

I was born and brought up in England, the youngest of three children. My wife and I got married at 21, and we are still very happily married. Unfortunately, on the day we got married my father died. My mother became both an "empty nester" and a widow on the same day. Fortunately, my wife and I had purchased a house that was close to my mother's home and also close to my wife's parents.

At 23, we had our first child, and shortly thereafter we moved to another house. Luckily, the new house was still quite close to my mother and my wife's parents. When we had our second child at 25, we moved house yet again. Nevertheless, we were still close by our families. However, within two months of that move, I was offered another job: a job that I really wanted. It was a real step up the career ladder for me. This time it meant that we had to move from England to Wales. Despite this, we were still only a two- or three-hour drive from our parents.

At age 27 we had our third child, and within about 18 months of that, my company offered me a position at its UK headquarters in the southern part of England, and we moved again. It was a little further away from our parents than our last house, but it seemed right to make the move because, once again, it would benefit my career. It would give me the international experience that I craved, as one of my key career goals was to get a position located overseas. I was determined to get the experience I needed so that I could ultimately secure such an overseas position with a high level of responsibility and a commensurate level of compensation before I was 30.

Then it happened.

At 29 years of age, I was offered an overseas position with another multinational company. It was a very significant career move for me. It would provide me with the level of responsibility and compensation I had been striving for. I really wanted the job. But this time it involved moving to what must have seemed to our parents like "the other end of the earth." It was in Kenya, in East Africa. I accepted the position and promptly moved with my wife and three children to Nairobi, the capital of Kenya.

Kenya was certainly a long way from England, but I didn't seem to care. I was extremely ambitious. I really wanted this career move. I justified it in my mind as being essential to ensure the future financial security of our family.

As I look back on that time in my life, I don't think that I ever truly considered the impact that this move would have on my mother and my wife's parents. I was so convinced that this move was important to my success in life that I believe I approached it with blind determination. I was ambitious. I was prepared to go anywhere to succeed in my chosen field.

I have since asked myself what gave me such a driving ambition. What was it that made me so willing to leave my widowed mother, my wife's parents, and all of our family and friends? I had an all-consuming desire to be successful in my career. It was pure ambition.

Reflecting about this apparently selfish ambition makes me wonder about the families that were left behind by the apostles. We know that at least some of them were married, including Peter. How did they feel about leaving their wives and families to follow Jesus, the carpenter from Nazareth—the man who delivered extraordinary and sometimes challenging teachings about what people needed to do in order to be saved?

I have to believe that the reality is that the apostles each had an all-consuming desire: an ambition to seek out the Messiah that had been promised to the Jewish people. It must have been this desire—this overwhelming ambition—that enabled them to readily accept the invitation of Jesus to follow him. It must have been something that they almost felt compelled to do, just as my ambition and blind determination seemed to have driven me to pursue my career almost irrespective of the cost to me, and, perhaps, more particularly, irrespective of the cost to my family. This had to be such a compulsion for the apostles that they were prepared to sacrifice everything, including being without their families and friends. They knew deep down that this was something that they had to do; they felt compelled to follow Jesus.

Why were the Apostles so committed? What made them this way, and why aren't most Christians today as committed as the Apostles were? Why isn't each of us today inflamed with a passion to hear and to spread the teachings of Jesus Christ, the Gospel, the Good News?

Why aren't we inflamed? Why don't we pursue the path to Heaven with as much fervor, ambition, and blind determination as we follow our worldly careers?

I wonder if, perhaps, a lot of Christians don't really understand what is so good about the so-called Good News. I wonder if the true message and meaning of God's incarnation and our salvation has been lost on many of us. I wonder how many Christians have not had the benefit of someone clearly articulating what is so good about what is contained in the gospels. If they had, surely they would not let anything or anyone stand between them and going out to spread the Good News.

Has our knowledge of the Good News had a profound impact on the way we live our lives? Has it resulted in us being even more committed to pursue the path towards Heaven, or are most of our ambitions still focused on the achievement of our worldly goals?

Travel Tip to Remember

Embrace an all-consuming desire to be successful in getting to Heaven by living the Good News of the Gospel. Be ambitious—ambitious for Heaven. Be absolutely committed to do whatever it takes on your part to achieve this goal and leave the rest to God. You can have every confidence that He will give you the grace and fortitude to accomplish that goal because that too is His goal for you.

Peter J. Moriarty

Matthew 25: 1 – 13

Then the kingdom of heaven will be like ten virgins who took their lamps and went out to meet the bridegroom. Five of them were foolish and five were wise. The foolish ones, when taking their lamps, brought no oil with them, but the wise brought flasks of oil with their lamps. Since the bridegroom was long delayed, they all became drowsy and fell asleep. At midnight, there was a cry, 'Behold, the bridegroom! Come out to meet him!' Then all those virgins got up and trimmed their lamps. The foolish ones said to the wise, 'Give us some of your oil, for our lamps are going out.' But the wise ones replied, 'No, for there may not be enough for us and you. Go instead to the merchants and buy some for yourselves.' While they went off to buy it, the bridegroom came and those who were ready went into the wedding feast with him. Then the door was locked. Afterwards the other virgins came and said, 'Lord, Lord, open the door for us!' But he said in reply, 'Amen, I say to you, I do not know you.' Therefore, stay awake, for you know neither the day nor the hour.

Chapter

11

I spent a great deal of my early life traveling to and living in a number of countries. One of the things that always fascinated me were the local customs with regard to politeness and social etiquette, which often differed quite dramatically from country to country.

For example, in Liberia, in West Africa, if you were experienced in the ways of the Liberians, you would ensure that when you shook hands with another person, each person would withdraw the hands from the clasp quite slowly and then click their fingers together.

In Norway, if you invited someone to a small party at your house and you opened a bottle of liquor, that person would not leave until the entire bottle was finished. (We would normally make sure that we brought out bottles that had already been partly or largely consumed, in order to avoid our guests getting terribly drunk.)

In Kenya, if you invited someone to a dinner party at your home starting at 7:00 pm, it was not unusual for the person to turn up at 8:00 pm, 8:30 pm, or even 9:00 pm. Their sense of time and promptness was entirely different to ours, and it was not done out of impoliteness. It was just the Kenyan way. It is not uncommon for guests to turn up for a wedding several hours or even a day late in Kenya.

On the other hand, in Demark if you invite someone to a dinner party at your home starting at 7:00 pm, it is not unusual for the person to arrive in your street at 6:45 pm and wait in their parked car so that they can knock on your door at precisely 7:00 pm. That is Danish etiquette: to be prepared and be on time.

Who is to say which country or culture is right and which is wrong? We are all different.

As Christians, we need to be prepared, just like the wise virgins in the gospels. As you may recall from the parable Christ told, there were five wise virgins who had taken the trouble to bring along oil for their lamps and five foolish ones who did not.

Of course, there are those people who are very wise and are probably always fully prepared to meet their Maker. Then there are others, perhaps many more, who feel that they are not yet ready, not yet prepared to meet their Heavenly Father. In my case, I know it's foolish. I know that I need to make improvements in my spiritual life and relationship with God, but I seem to find every excuse in the book to put off doing it. I am sure that many of us say to ourselves, "I will make that change or behave better when I have less going on in my life—less going on with work or with family issues or whatever." It's always easier to put off to tomorrow what really could, and should, be done today.

If we take the parable of the wise and foolish virgins to heart, what is our response? Each of us needs to ask ourselves if we are the type of person who consistently puts off making changes in their spiritual life—puts off making the improvements that only we know we need to make.

When it comes to being ready to meet your Maker, which nationality are you most like in terms of timeliness? Are you going to be prepared on time to meet your Heavenly Father, irrespective of when or where it happens?

Travel Tip to Remember
Always be prepared for your journey. Don't leave anything to chance because the end of the journey might come sooner than you expected.

Luke 22:24-26

Then an argument broke out among them about which of them should be regarded as the greatest. He said to them, "The kings of the Gentiles lord it over them and those in authority over them are addressed as 'Benefactors'; but among you it shall not be so. Rather, let the greatest among you be as the youngest, and the leader as the servant."

Mark 10:42-45

Jesus summoned them and said to them, "You know that those who are recognized as rulers over the Gentiles lord it over them, and their great ones make their authority over them felt. But it shall not be so among you. Rather, whoever wishes to be great among you will be your servant; whoever wishes to be first among you will be the slave of all. For the Son of Man did not come to be served but to serve and to give his life as a ransom for many."

Chapter

12

Living in Nairobi, Kenya, we followed the normal local practice of employing servants. In that country, it was quite normal. It provided necessary employment for the local people.

In fact, we employed three servants, and two of them lived in a couple of houses that we had on the grounds of our property. One day, when I was inside the main house, I heard an enormous commotion outside. It was our houseboy (the servant responsible for cooking, cleaning, etc.) having a very heated argument with our gardener— and I do mean "heated," which was most unusual.

I went outside to tell them to "cease and desist." However, it soon became clear that it was not going to be that easy. Ordering them to stop was not going to work.

Being British, I decided that the answer was "a nice cup of tea." (Just as you see in the old British colonial movies.) I then proceeded to tell them that I was going to make them each a cup of tea and that I was going to serve it to them. And that is exactly what I did…much to their surprise and amazement. I then told them that I wanted them to sit down together, enjoy the cup of tea, and quietly resolve their differences.

To my delight, and, frankly, my own amazement, the situation quickly calmed down. I realized that it was not so much the tea that had astounded them but the fact that I, the person they knew as the "Bwana Mkubwa," the "big boss," had made it and served it to them. It worked wonders. It seemed like a little miracle. It really brought home to me that even as the Bwana Mkubwa, whether it be the boss of a household or the boss of a company, we get much better results if we treat people with dignity, respect, and a genuine desire to seek the best for them—to serve them rather than trying to "lord it over them."

That is one of the key messages in the New Testament. Those who wish to lead must take on the responsibility of the servant. Our duty is to serve our fellow man.

We all have opportunities to lead others by serving them, and many do precisely that. They go out of their way, and out of their comfort zone, to serve others. I frequently ask myself if I have done enough for others, and, unfortunately, my answer more often than not comes back as a resounding "No." I realize that I have not made the big sacrifices that others seem to have made.

I suspect that many of us feel that we could do more for our fellow man. Furthermore, I don't suppose that it has to be something big. Perhaps it's more to do with changing our attitude to our fellow man—not thinking that we are better than others—seeing the face of Christ in everyone that we encounter—finding ways, even little ways, of positively impacting the life of others, no matter who they are, where they are from, or whatever they have done. It is only by properly appreciating that we are all God's children that we will consistently reach out to help others, whether it is in big or little ways.

As Mother Teresa once said, "Few of us can do great things, but all of us can do small things with great love." That should be an inspiration to all of us.

Travel Tip to Remember
Our mission in life is to serve others. We are all God's children. Therefore, we have a duty to help other members of God's family, no matter who they are, where they are from, or what they have done. Try to always remember that we each have family responsibilities as children of God. Remember that it doesn't have to be big acts of kindness but rather consistent acts of kindness.

Peter J. Moriarty

Mark 12:28-31

One of the scribes, when he came forward and heard them disputing and saw how well he had answered them, asked him, "Which is the first of all the commandments?" Jesus replied, "The first is this: 'Hear, O Israel! The Lord our God is Lord alone! You shall love the Lord your God with all your heart, with all your soul, with all your mind, and with all your strength.' The second is this: 'You shall love your neighbor as yourself.' There is no other commandment greater than these."

Chapter

13

I want to tell you about two events that have impacted my life. The first happened many years ago. The second is far more recent.

The first event happened in Kenya when I was out in a game reserve with my family. We were looking for lions. We spotted some circling vultures in the sky and went off the dirt track into the bush to find the carcass of the dead animal that was obviously in the area. We knew that if we found the carcass we would probably find the lions or possibly a cheetah.

We found the well-eaten carcass of a wildebeest but could not see any lions. We searched and searched but without success. Eventually, I stopped our vehicle and announced to my family that I was getting out of the car and going to have a quick look around on foot to see if I could spot a lion.

I got out of the vehicle and almost trod on a sleeping lioness. I was so close that if I had put one foot out of place, I would have been dessert. However, it was sleeping soundly, having fed well on the fallen wildebeest.

It was a stupid thing to do: to get out of the car. The lion was so close that I couldn't see it. I was looking way beyond where it was.

I think that the event with the lion taught me that I, and many other people, can spend our whole lives looking for God but perhaps don't see Him because we are looking too far afield. We are looking in distant places when God is really right next to us. He is close by, and we just fail to see Him. In fact, He is so close that we can almost fall over Him. We are sometimes looking so hard but in all the wrong places. God is in the simple places. He is sitting next to us in the pew. He is in the heart of the homeless person that we pass on the street. He is in the heart, believe it or not, of the person or persons we find most difficult to like or love.

The second and more recent event occurred when I woke up in the middle of the night with the following words running through my mind: "You cannot love God unless you love other people." It nagged at me and has stayed with me since, reminding me that it is my obligation as a child of God to love my fellow man: all of God's other children.

It now is clear to me that it is impossible to truly love God unless we really take action to love our fellow man. We can do all the praying and attending church that we want, but if we do not show love to our fellow man, it makes our practice of Christianity basically meaningless.

One might almost say that "God is other people." Everything that Jesus taught us directs us towards loving God with our whole hearts, our whole minds, and our whole beings, but it also directs us to love our neighbor: our fellow man.

We cannot truly love God unless that love overflows to true, demonstrated love of our neighbor, no matter who they are, where they are from, or what they have done. It is an obligation—not a choice—but I have to admit that I sometimes find it very hard to put it into practice. Unfortunately, I sometimes seem to only engage in it in a half-hearted manner.

However, just to put it into perspective, I am constantly fascinated by the good work done by the likes of Bono, Bill and Melinda Gates, and other high-profile people. They reach out to make a real difference in the world, particularly with regard to the millions of starving people in the third world who are plagued not only by hunger and famine but also by a lack of healthcare and an overwhelming amount of poverty, disease, and discomfort. I ease my conscience about not doing anything myself to help people in the third world by telling myself that I can't compete with these high-profile celebrities—I don't have the resources that they have.

But that's just an excuse, and I know it.

I don't really do much about the suffering in the world, even in a small way. I leave it to others. I have every excuse possible, and that's just not good enough. As a child of God and a professed follower of Jesus Christ, I know that I am obligated to care for my fellow man: to go out of my way to relieve suffering, despair, hunger, and illness.

For most of us, taking real action to help our fellow man takes more courage than most of us believe we have. For most of us, we are too comfortable in our daily routines to break out and do something that will really make a difference. We are too frightened of what others might think: our families, our friends, our colleagues at work.

We just need to take that first step. We need to ask God to give us the courage to take that first step towards helping our fellow man in some concrete fashion. Remember that God is there to help. God is nearby. In fact, he is so close that we could almost step on Him. He is there to help us overcome our fears and our apprehensions about doing something that is beyond our comfort zone: to show our love for Him by the way we love His other children.

Travel Tip to Remember

It's no use professing to be a Christian if all you do is go to church and participate in religious rituals. Seek God and pursue God's ways. However, you first have to stop looking for God as though He is a long way off. Be aware that He is nearby—close enough to step on. Don't be afraid to step outside of your comfort zone in an all-out effort to take meaningful actions to help your fellow man. God is other people.

"WAY to go!"

Jeremiah 18:6

Can I not do to you, house of Israel, as this potter has done?—oracle of the LORD. Indeed, like clay in the hand of the potter, so are you in my hand, house of Israel.

Matthew 13:47-49

Again, the kingdom of heaven is like a net thrown into the sea, which collects fish of every kind. When it is full they haul it ashore and sit down to put what is good into buckets. What is bad they throw away. Thus it will be at the end of the age. The angels will go out and separate the wicked from the righteous.

Chapter

14

I love women. Well, I love most things about women. There are a couple of things that I am not so comfortable with…but I do love women. So why don't I start with telling you what I am not comfortable with.

It's not that I am uncomfortable as much as it seems unfair that women have great intuition. They can see right through you. There's no putting on an act with a woman. In fact, with one of my earlier businesses, I always had a female senior executive interview final candidates for senior positions. The female executive's intuition was always so much better than mine.

Take the case of a husband and wife. The wife always seems to know what the husband is thinking. In fact, my wife sometimes answers me before I have even asked the question. I've asked her how she does that, and she has told me that "somehow" she always seems to know what I am thinking. That is what I am not so comfortable with.

Now let me tell you what I really love about women.

I love their ability to love unconditionally. Just look at the way they treat our children. It doesn't matter whether it's a tot, a teen, or a very trying adult child, the mother always loves her child unconditionally. No matter what the child does wrong, even if there are fallouts and vehement disagreements, the mother always loves that child unconditionally.

If you think about it, God always knows what we are thinking, even before we have thought those thoughts. God knows what is best for us and will always do what is best, rather than just granting us what we want—just like a mother. And God always loves us unconditionally, no matter how many times we go wrong. God is always there for us, helping to get us back on track and helping us to reshape our lives.

I suppose that God's unconditional love for us has been depicted in many ways throughout the Old and the New Testaments. For example, in the Old Testament, in the Book of Jeremiah, we read that God is rather like a potter, working with his hands to shape and mold the clay spinning round on his potter's wheel. Whenever something goes wrong with the shape of the clay, the potter tries again. He never gives up no matter how many times it goes wrong. The potter sticks with shaping the clay until he creates the perfection that he is looking for.

In Matthew 13, we read that at the end of the world, the bad fish will be discarded and only the good fish will be saved. However, it is important that we understand this in terms of our knowledge that God, like the potter, never gives up on us—that God will be with us throughout our lives to ensure that we turn out to be the beautiful creations that He wants us to be: the good fish. It doesn't matter how many times we go wrong, it doesn't matter how grievous we think our sins are, if we go back to God with determination to do better in the future, God will always give us the grace and power to become perfect: to become the beautiful creations He wants and we want to be. God always knows what we want. God knows what is good for us and loves us unconditionally. We should take great comfort in that.

Travel Tip to Remember

God never gives up on us. He is like the potter who sticks with shaping the clay until he creates the perfection that he is looking for. It doesn't matter how many times we go wrong, or how grievous we think our sins are, if we go back to God with determination to do better in the future, God will always give us the grace and power to become the beautiful creations He wants us to be.

Peter J. Moriarty

Psalm 23

The LORD is my shepherd;
there is nothing I lack.
In green pastures he makes me lie down;
to still waters he leads me;
he restores my soul.
He guides me along right paths
for the sake of his name.
Even though I walk through the valley of the shadow of
death,
I will fear no evil, for you are with me;
your rod and your staff comfort me.
You set a table before me
in front of my enemies;
You anoint my head with oil;
my cup overflows.
Indeed, goodness and mercy will pursue me
all the days of my life;
I will dwell in the house of the LORD
for endless days.

Chapter

15

Some years ago, the newspapers announced that a very large pharmaceutical company was going to lay off 20% of its US sales force. That meant that about 2,200 sales people were going to lose their jobs just around Christmas time. That's not very pleasant for anybody. The trouble is that the pharmaceutical industry is renowned for "acting like sheep." Therefore, once that news was announced, it was almost inevitable that there would be even more layoffs in the industry. Once one major company does something, others tend to follow. It's as though every other company is sitting back and waiting to see what its competitors are going to do. Then when one makes a move, they all follow. However, up until that point everyone is afraid to make the first move even if they know what needs to be done to improve performance.

When I think about the phrase "follow like sheep," my first thought is that it is somewhat of an insult—that I am using that phrase in a rather a pejorative or insulting manner. I would hate anybody to think that my company was a follower. It is rather an insult. It implies mindlessness, gutlessness, and not thinking for oneself. I would prefer to be seen as a leader.

So are the words of the Psalm, "The Lord is my shepherd," in conflict with this view of the world?

We hear the beautiful words "The Lord is my shepherd. There is nothing I shall want." I don't think that there is anyone, at least that I know of, who does not have a particular affection for that Psalm. Yet I ask the question, "Doesn't the Psalm imply that we are to be mere mindless sheep following our Shepherd, Christ, our Lord and our Savior?"

No. I don't think that even for one minute. It's just a beautiful image of the caring, loving leader. The servant of all that follow him. The leader who will lead his followers to success and risk his life to protect them from any danger that may be encountered. The leader who thinks in terms of the individual. The leader who will go out of his way to rescue any one of his followers who gets lost along the way, no matter how low and how humble their position is in life.

Now isn't that unusual nowadays: having a leader we can trust—one who will lead his or her followers to success and risk their own life to protect them from danger.

Isn't this beautiful and comforting? It's very different from the business world. It's what Christianity is all about. Leadership is a Christian virtue, if practiced correctly. It's about always putting others before oneself. It's about putting one's ego aside and being selfless. It's about serving others. It's about going out of one's way to help everyone, even, and perhaps especially, those on the margins of society who are invisible to many.

The image of Christ, the Good Shepherd, provides us with the supreme example of great leadership, whether it is in the religious life of our church, the big world of business, or just being a family leader as a parent.

It doesn't matter how many business training courses we take, Psalm 23 may contain the best set of leadership guidelines that any of us could have. This is what being a good leader is all about.

None of us would have a problem following like sheep if we had absolute confidence that the shepherd, the leader, really was putting his or her ego aside, and seeing that their role was that of our defender, our protector, putting our interests above their own or someone else higher up in their hierarchy. This is what we should expect of leaders, and it is our responsibility, whenever and wherever we are a leader, to follow Christ's example in the way we treat those we lead, whether that be in the church, in our business, or in our homes.

Travel Tip to Remember
Always put others before yourself. Put your ego aside. Selflessly, find ways of going out of your way to help everyone, even, and perhaps especially, those on the margins of society whom the world seems to shun.

Peter J. Moriarty

Luke 1:30

Then the angel said to her, "Do not be afraid, Mary, for you have found favor with God."

Chapter

16

Just think for a minute about what the word "humiliation" means to you, particularly in the context of feeling that you have let someone down.

When I was in corporate life, I had a reputation as someone who got things done, particularly when the odds were against me. When I was transferred from an overseas position to my company's global headquarters in New Jersey, I was given responsibility in a brand-new area. One of my key undertakings was of very great importance to the president of our division. In fact, it was the president who had selected me to get this particular innovation accomplished on an international basis.

After about a year or so of working with an outside company, helping them design a system that would meet my company's needs, and lining up key international subsidiaries of our company to undertake pilot testing of the new system whenever it was completed, I received some disturbing news. The outside company that had been developing the system informed me that they were "pulling the plug" on the project. They were discontinuing their development.

Well, you can imagine how I felt. I was embarrassed. I felt humiliated. I felt that I had let down the president, who had entrusted this high-profile project to me. I had not been able to successfully accomplish what had been expected of me.

Has anything like that ever happened to you? Have you ever felt really humiliated, particularly when what went wrong appeared to be totally beyond your control? If so, just think for a minute about how you felt.

Now contrast that with the New Testament story of Mary, the Mother of Jesus, who was visited by an angel and told that she was chosen by God to give birth to a very special baby, the Messiah, the savior the Jewish people had been waiting for: the chosen one, the Holy one of God.

Then several months later, Mary learned that she and her husband Joseph had to leave their home town of Nazareth to register for the census being conducted by the Romans. I imagine that she had been preparing their home for the birth of their child, and then she found out that they had to travel when she was very pregnant—not a particularly pleasant proposition.

Of course, on the way back from registering in the census, Mary told Joseph that she could feel that the baby was on the way. She couldn't go any further. She couldn't make it home.

She told Joseph that he had better find a room where she could have some privacy and warmth while she gave birth to the baby. After all, any woman would want privacy, warmth, and cleanliness.

And what happened? Joseph couldn't get a room. There was not one to be had in the town. There was nowhere where she could give birth to the Son of God in privacy. Instead, the only place she could go to was a hovel, a cave, a shelter for animals—a place probably full of animals, hay, dung, and all the smells that we would associate with such a place.

How humiliated she must have felt. She must have felt that she was letting God down. She could not even make it back to her own home, where she had been preparing and planning to have the child. Instead, she had no choice but to give birth to our Savior in an animal shelter.

I think that it is important to remember that God so loved us that he freely came into the world under the most humiliating of circumstances. Likewise, when he left the world, he did so by dying under the most humiliating of circumstances: death on the cross. Crucifixion was, in those days, considered the worst of executions, reserved for those considered to be "the cursed of God."

God, in the form of Jesus, our Lord and our Savior, physically came into the world in humiliation—and physically left the world in humiliation.

I think that God was trying to tell us something. I think that he was trying to send us a message in His birth and His death—a message that we should find very comforting.

God loves us so much that he subjected himself to the worst of humiliations so that we could always know and take comfort in the fact that He has "been there and done that." In our most desperate of moments (and we all have those moments at some time in our lives), we can absolutely trust that God knows how we are feeling and is with us, perhaps even more intently. Perhaps in our greatest moments of pain, physical and mental, God is truly with us, understanding us, and stretching out an arm to comfort us.

Perhaps this is one of the greatest "wonders of the world": that God our Almighty Father would humble himself so much for us.

Travel Tip to Remember
When you are feeling pain, humiliation, embarrassment, disillusionment, despair, or deep sorrow, take comfort in knowing that God is with you. Know that He understands what you are going through and will give you the grace and courage to get through it. Remember that He has been there Himself. He, in the form of Jesus, came into the world in humiliation and left the world in humiliation, having physically suffered for our salvation.

"WAY to go!"

Peter J. Moriarty

John 20:11-17

But Mary stayed outside the tomb weeping. And as she wept, she bent over into the tomb and saw two angels in white sitting there, one at the head and one at the feet where the body of Jesus had been. And they said to her, "Woman, why are you weeping?" She said to them, "They have taken my Lord, and I don't know where they laid him." When she had said this, she turned around and saw Jesus there, but did not know it was Jesus. Jesus said to her, "Woman, why are you weeping? Whom are you looking for?" She thought it was the gardener and said to him, "Sir, if you carried him away, tell me where you laid him, and I will take him." Jesus said to her, "Mary!" She turned and said to him in Hebrew, "Rabbouni," which means Teacher. Jesus said to her, "Stop holding on to me, for I have not yet ascended to the Father. But go to my brothers and tell them, 'I am going to my Father and your Father, to my God and your God.'"

Acts 2:36-39

Therefore let the whole house of Israel know for certain that God has made him both Lord and Messiah, this Jesus whom you crucified."
Now when they heard this, they were cut to the heart, and they asked Peter and the other apostles, "What are we to do, my brothers?" Peter [said] to them, "Repent and be baptized, every one of you, in the name of Jesus Christ for the forgiveness of your sins; and you will receive the gift of the holy Spirit. For the promise is made to you and to your children and to all those far off, whomever the Lord our God will call."

Chapter

17

On the day that I got married, my father died. I was devastated. I thought that I had lost so much with his death. Yet I found over time that he had left me with so much. It was as if his soul lived on. The essence of the things that he had taught me—the example that he had given me—all have played a big part in the way I conduct my life since his death.

When I was a little boy, I was an altar server. I would have to perform my duties at early morning mass for a week each month. What I do remember from that is that our family doctor was always at mass. He always went to mass before he started seeing patients. That image really burned into me. That was many, many years ago, and yet I still think about it. I often think how smart it was for him to place himself before God every day before he began his work. I am absolutely sure that he had no idea what a positive impression he was making on that little altar server. But all those years later, his example lives on.

In the New Testament, we read of Mary Magdalene's encounter when she found that the body of Jesus was missing from the tomb. She had already been devastated by the physical loss of Jesus. She clearly felt that she had lost everything and yet subsequently found that he had left her, and the rest of us, so much. His living and his dying created a resurrection in all of us to move from death to everlasting life, if we will but follow His example and His teachings.

You may also recall that in the Acts of the Apostles the Jews, in realization of what had happened to Jesus and in the realization that he was the Messiah, asked, "What are we to do, my Brothers?" St. Peter replied, "Repent and be baptized…." This means put your past behind you and follow the teachings of Jesus, who was and is your Messiah. Essentially, what St. Peter was saying was that they had to change the way they led their lives. That was and is the true sign of "repentance." They had to listen and learn from the teachings and example of Jesus.

The same is true for us. Think about the example Jesus gave us in the way he led his life. Think about the essence of what He taught his disciples. His core message, the essence of what He wanted to impart to them, was, "Love the Father with your whole heart, your whole soul, your whole mind, and with all of your strength, and let that love overflow to love of your neighbor no matter who they are, where they are from or whatever they have done to you or to others. Love them. Love each other."

We have to banish selfishness from our lives. We have to realize that the way we lead our lives impacts other people, whether or not we realize that. We have much more of an influence on other people than most of us realize: both positive and negative. The way we act, the things we say, the things we don't say, the demeanor we display, the care and concern that we genuinely show for others, the irritations, the anger, and the "tittle tattle" that we engage in—all of these things influence other people. Sometimes we influence others in a positive way, and sometimes, unfortunately, we influence them in a very negative way. The worst part about it is that most of us often don't realize the influence we have on others. For most of the time, we don't realize that people are watching and taking note of what we say or do, both consciously and unconsciously. If we did, I am sure that most of us would try to have a positive influence and go out of our way to make sure that the influence is not negative.

Our impact on others is enormous.

I, therefore, want you to consider the following question:

If you or I were arrested today for being a Christian, would we be convicted?

Would the prosecution be able to amass enough evidence against us to prove, beyond a reasonable shadow of doubt, that you and I are followers of the teachings of Jesus Christ?

Would the prosecution be able to bring forward enough people to give concrete, not circumstantial, evidence, that you and I really have been leading a life that follows the actual teachings of Jesus Christ?

Travel Tip to Remember
Make a daily commitment to be mindful of the fact that the way you behave, the things you say (and the things you don't say), your whole demeanor, and the genuine care and concern you show for others will have a direct and positive influence on other people, including people who you may not realize are being exposed to your words and deeds. It's up to you whether your words and actions have a positive or a negative impact on those people. Ask

Peter J. Moriarty

yourself the question, "If I were arrested today for being an obvious Christian, would I be convicted?"

"WAY to go!"

Luke 1:30-38

Then the angel said to her, "Do not be afraid, Mary, for you have found favor with God. Behold, you will conceive in your womb and bear a son, and you shall name him Jesus. He will be great and will be called Son of the Most High, and the Lord God will give him the throne of David his father, and he will rule over the house of Jacob forever, and of his kingdom there will be no end." But Mary said to the angel, "How can this be, since I have no relations with a man?" And the angel said to her in reply, "The holy Spirit will come upon you, and the power of the Most High will overshadow you. Therefore the child to be born will be called holy, the Son of God. And behold, Elizabeth, your relative, has also conceived a son in her old age, and this is the sixth month for her who was called barren; for nothing will be impossible for God." Mary said, "Behold, I am the handmaid of the Lord. May it be done to me according to your word." Then the angel departed from her.

Chapter

18

One night, while I lay in bed, I started thinking of the high-profile people I look up to the most or, probably more accurately, those who have impressed me the most. I decided that they are Mother Theresa, Mahatma Gandhi, and Jimmy Carter.

I then realized that they all have something in common.

Mother Theresa was called to be a missionary nun. She left her native Yugoslavia to be a teacher in a school in Calcutta. She subsequently responded to another call from God, which was to go out onto the streets of Calcutta to love and care for the poor.

Mahatma Gandhi was called to be an attorney in South Africa and subsequently received another call to lead the great nation of India to independence, succeeding against all odds to peacefully overcome colonial rule.

Jimmy Carter was called to ascend to the highest office in the United States, becoming our 39th president. He was subsequently called by God to have perhaps a much greater impact on the world after his presidency. His post-presidency humanitarian activities have been a great example to all Americans and many others in the world. He has clearly demonstrated the importance and impact that selfless acts of service can have on our fellow man.

I believe that these are all great people who carried out their high-profile callings with a great deal of humility and showed their humbleness of heart on the world stage.

But what struck me most about all three of these people is that, despite what might have seemed like a definitive earlier calling, they each received a subsequent calling to which they positively responded and have had, in my view, a deep and meaningful impact on the world.

I think that it is most important that we are all open to listening to God's calling, no matter what age we are and no matter what "calling" we are currently engaged in. We have to be attentive to God. We have to listen to Him because He might well have another calling to which He wants us to respond. We need to spend quiet time with God, listen for His calling, and be prepared to say "Yes," no matter what it is.

Just look at Mary, the mother of Jesus. There she was, a teenage girl, betrothed to be married to Joseph, and then she got a visit from an angel who told her that God had chosen her—God had called her to give birth to, and take responsibility for raising, the Messiah, the holy one of God. That must have been quite a shock. She was just a young girl who had kept herself pure and holy. Now she was going to have to tell her family and her fiancé that she was pregnant. She was going to have to try to convince them that she was still pure and holy, and, perhaps, what is even more of a challenge is that she was going to have to try to convince them that this was some heavenly event. She was going to have to convince them that the Holy Spirit was responsible for her pregnancy and that she, this young and vulnerable teenager, had been chosen to be the mother of the One who would save the world.

And so what did she do? She placed her trust in God. She said "Yes" to God, no matter what the cost to her in terms of embarrassment, ridicule, and uncertainty of the future.

Could you and I do that?

Do we listen to God?

Are we open to hearing God's calling and open to responding positively to it, no matter what our age or what we think we have or have not already achieved in life?

Let's hope that we could all be a little like Mary and respond positively to God's calling, no matter the consequences.

Perhaps we can take comfort from people like Mother Theresa, Mahatma Gandhi, and Jimmy Carter. They thought they knew their calling in life but were open to a new calling and responded positively and with great humility, even on the world stage.

Travel Tip to Remember
Take time to be silent with God. Get rid of other distractions from your mind. Take time to listen to Him. Make a deliberate decision to be open to His calling whatever it might entail. Be ready to say "Yes." It might be frightening, but it might also be the road that God wants you to follow to ensure you reach Heaven.

Peter J. Moriarty

John 3:29-30

The one who has the bride is the bridegroom; the best man, who stands and listens to him, rejoices greatly at the bridegroom's voice. So this joy of mine has been made complete. He must increase; I must decrease.

Chapter

19

Some years ago, I worked with someone who was always taking credit for projects or work for which he was not totally responsible. He was consistently expounding on how "he" had done this or "he" had done that when it was his team who had done it. On other occasions, he had hardly been associated with the work at all. He just seemed to be compelled to insert himself into the project if it was successful. "I did this" or "I did that." There was never any mention of the other people who really did the work.

What used to frustrate me was that, in other respects, he was a very nice person. He just had a bad habit taking credit for other people's work. I presumed that it was the manifestation of some sort of inferiority complex. It was always about him. "I, I, I." It was never about "We." "We" was not part of his vocabulary, and he rarely gave any credit to others unless it involved him looking as though he were the "king pin" and the person really responsible for success. It seemed very self-centered—very selfish.

On the other hand, another person with whom I worked was the exact opposite. He always talked about living by the "single cookie" rule—his personal rule—the rule that if you have one cookie and someone else is hungry, then you give it to them. If you only have one cookie and many people are hungry, give them each a piece of it, and don't be selfish. Don't try to leave a few crumbs for yourself.

What I always find interesting about this "single cookie" person is that he has no particular religious affiliation. He is a Christian but certainly never goes to a place of worship. However, he lives his life as a true Christian, trying to be selfless and doing as much as possible to bring joy into the lives of others.

At one point, I discussed his "single cookie rule" with him, and he told me that many years ago he had decided that he was not going to focus on being a so-called "winner"—or, at least not the sort of "winner" to which most people in this world refer. He said that he had decided that he was going to focus on being kind to others: helping others to be happy and helping them to achieve their full potential. Then he said to me, "And do you know what? Since I started to live my life in that way, I have experienced real joy and happiness in my own life."

What a great example.

Unfortunately, however, I think he might be somewhat of an exception in today's world. I think that most of us have a slight tendency towards selfishness: a tendency to want to be noticed. Our lives are somewhat centered around "I."

This makes me realize again that selfishness is perhaps the greatest manifestation of original sin. It is exactly the opposite of the way God wants us to lead our lives; God wants us to be selfless.

In the New Testament, John the Baptist recognized that Jesus was the promised Messiah. Jesus was now going to be "the star of the show," not John. And what was John's reaction? It was one of selflessness. John was delighted, as evidenced in the words:

"So this joy of mine has been made complete.
He must increase; I must decrease."

This is a beautiful guideline for all of us in our dealings with others:

- Never do things at the expense of others.
- Always put others before ourselves.
- There is no place for selfishness in God's kingdom.
- Selflessness is the way of God.

Travel Tip to Remember
Live by the "single cookie" rule. Be selfless and not selfish; don't ever try to steal the credit that is due to others.

Peter J. Moriarty

Hebrews 7:25

Therefore, he is always able to save those who approach God through him, since he lives forever to make intercession for them.

Mark 3:11

And whenever unclean spirits saw him they would fall down before him and shout, "You are the Son of God."

Chapter

20

A few years ago, I received an email from a friend from my boarding school days. I had not seen my friend since just before I got married, which was nearly forty years earlier. Apparently, he had located me by searching for me through an online business directory. The strange thing is that only the week before he contacted me I had a dream in which I met up with him.

In replying to my friend's email, I asked him to bring me up to date with what had happened in his life over the years since I had last seen him. He decided to respond by writing his life in chapters: a few years at a time.

I learned that he had been married for many years. He and his wife had had five children, one of whom had died as a baby. Clearly, the image that I had of him now, through the contents of his email, was that of a stable, conservative family man. This was clearly not the person I had previously known. That was very intriguing to me. When I had last known him, he was going through his "Marxist revolutionary" phase. He was in his early twenties, and he seemed to have abandoned all formal religious practices. He appeared to be focused on all that was "extreme left wing." From what I read in the chapters of the email he sent me, he had clearly had periods of torment, pain and sorrow, which had then been followed by periods of joy and happiness, followed by periods of pain and sorrow, and so forth.

So what's so different about this? The answer is "nothing." This is the normal ebb and flow of life. It's just that we sometimes forget that it is happening to most other people and not only to us.

However, the thing that struck me most when reading the various chapters of my friend's life was that each was just a few sentences long. Here he was taking the trouble to note the key experiences of the various stages of his life, and he did it very well. I thought to myself, "He reminds me of God." He was able to see life concisely. He didn't bother with the extraneous things. He focused only on the things that really mattered, and I am sure that God must look at things in a similar way.

God sees all of our experiences, our ups our downs, our successes and our failures, and yet He judges us by our lives as a whole: by what our life adds up to, and not by our individual failings and shortcomings. God sees the ebbs and flows of our lives. He sees the many good things we do probably far more so than the bad things we are responsible for. I believe that God takes the so-called "helicopter view." He judges us by our complete lives. He knows our sorrows and our joys, our pain and our happiness, but perhaps more particularly, I think he focuses on what we make of our lives. He sees the goodness in all of us, and even though we may have areas of darkness, in God's eyes, that darkness is overcome by the light we create with the goodness that we do.

The challenge for most of us is that we sometimes get so engrossed in the minutia of our lives that we fail to see the big picture. We focus on the extraneous matters. We feel so sorry for ourselves when we are going through periods of pain or sadness that we forget that happiness will return. We don't think about the fact that when bad things happen, they happen for a good reason, and good things come of them. We get so desperate that we forget the ebb and flow of life. We forget that inevitably daylight follows darkness. It just sometimes takes longer than we think it should. We want immediate relief. But happiness does come. We just seem to push this to the back of our minds when all we can think about is, "Why is this happening to me?"

In the New Testament, we are often given a "wake-up call": a reminder that, no matter what our state of mind, no matter what our fortunes or misfortunes in life, we always have God and we always have Jesus, the son of God. We read in the Letter to the Hebrews that Jesus "is always able to save those who approach God through him." Even the unclean spirits fell down before Jesus and proclaimed, "You are the Son of God."

God is the one constant in our lives. We always have Him in the bad times as well as in the good times. He can heal our pain and our sorrows. He can soothe our anxieties. He can eliminate our worries. He can bring us great happiness and consolation. However, we first have to acknowledge God and acknowledge that Jesus is the Son of God, as did the unclean spirits.

Travel Tip to Remember
Live your life as perfectly as you can, but always appreciate that God is pure love and that He takes the "helicopter view." He sees your complete life, and not just any faults you might have, and He judges you accordingly.

Peter J. Moriarty

Remember that the light of your goodness can overcome any darkness. Be a light to the world in your own unique way, and always trust in God and His son, Jesus, the Christ.

"WAY to go!"

Peter J. Moriarty

Philippians 2:3-4

Do nothing out of selfishness or out of vainglory; rather, humbly regard others as more important than yourselves, each looking out not for his own interests, but [also] everyone for those of others.

James 3:16

For where jealousy and selfish ambition exist, there is disorder and every foul practice.

Chapter

21

Both before and while I lived in Kenya, I traveled extensively throughout the African continent, visiting Tanzania, Ethiopia, Somalia, Zimbabwe, Mozambique, South Africa, Nigeria, Ghana, Sierra Leone, and Liberia. After living in Kenya for a number of years, my company moved me to Denmark, and then subsequently to Norway, and then finally to the United States.

Each time I was preparing to move to another country, and even when I was just preparing for regular visits to a country, I tried to spend as much time as possible learning about the country, its people, their customs, practices, languages, and traditions. In particular, I wanted to learn what made the people different. I wanted to make sure that I fitted in as much and as soon as possible.

Now, as I reach that stage in my life where I need to think more about my next great journey, a journey that will, hopefully, take me to the Kingdom of Heaven, I realize that I need to treat my preparation for this journey, whenever it will happen, just as I would if I were going to live in another country. I need to learn as much as possible about Heaven well in advance—to try to discover what the people in Heaven might really be like. I need to think seriously about how those people, those souls, must behave. I need to meditate on what makes them different from us on earth. I need to think seriously about what I can do now to properly prepare myself and ensure that I am fit for that heavenly Kingdom, and, in reality, to ensure that I actually arrive in the right place!

Have you ever thought about Heaven in those terms?

I realized some time ago that this thought process might help me to focus on the really important things that I need to do to prepare for Heaven instead of worrying about all those incidental, man-made sins or transgressions that bothered me as a child.

Anyway, the more I thought, read, and prayed about it, I was amazed by the simplicity of what I concluded.

I started with the premise that being in Heaven means being with God. It's His country: His Kingdom. He is the King. The inhabitants must therefore act in ways that are acceptable to Him. So what ways are acceptable to God, the King of Heaven?

Well, we know that God is pure love—a love so great and so giving that it overflowed to create us: Mankind. A love that further manifested itself by God coming among us in the form of Jesus Christ to teach us and lead us to eternal life in the Kingdom.

We also know that the central theme of Jesus' teaching was that in order to be fit for the Kingdom of Heaven we have to love the Lord our God with our whole heart and our whole being, but we also absolutely have to love our neighbor. We have to put others before ourselves. We have to stop being selfish. That is the way of the Kingdom of God. That is the culture of Heaven.

Have you ever really thought long and deeply about selfishness?

I did, and I came to realize that basically all of my many shortcomings are totally rooted in selfishness. I could not believe how much of what I think, do, and say each day is really rooted in an innate desire to think first and foremost about myself. Basically, all of my failings are rooted in my desire to please, protect, provide for, or promote myself.

My conclusion is that selfishness is the underlying problem with humanity and that it is probably selfishness that most differentiates those of us on earth from those who are already in the Kingdom of Heaven.

I believe that if we want to be ready for Heaven, we absolutely must do everything possible to get rid of our selfishness. We have to become selfless. By loving others, we clearly show our love for God.

Selfishness is a killer. It's what makes mankind so cruel. It's what brings about our impurities, our aggression, our wars, our sorrows. By focusing on the elimination of selfishness above all things, I believe that we can truly prepare for the greatest journey of our lives: our travel to the Kingdom of Heaven.

Travel Tip to Remember
The single most destructive force in this world is man's intrinsic selfishness. It is what differentiates us on earth from those in Heaven. If we want to ensure a safe and successful trip to Heaven, we need to practice unmitigated acts of selflessness on a daily basis.

Luke 1:26-30

In the sixth month, the angel Gabriel was sent from God to a town of Galilee called Nazareth, a virgin betrothed to a man named Joseph, of the house of David, and the virgin's name was Mary. And coming to her, he said, "Hail, favored one! The Lord is with you." But she was greatly troubled at what was said and pondered what sort of greeting this might be. Then the angel said to her, "Do not be afraid, Mary, for you have found favor with God."

Chapter

22

Do you ever feel that life is getting on top of you? That you are besieged by problems? Problems related to work, finances, relationships, health, or family? Do you ever think to yourself, "What have I done to deserve this?"

I am sure that this happens to most of us at some time or another, and when it happens, some people begin to doubt their own self-worth. It's at those moments of despair and despondency that we have a tendency to say to ourselves, "If God is prepared to let this happen to me, I cannot be very valuable in God's eyes." "If God has a plan for me, it sure seems to be going wrong," or "I am way down on God's totem pole." "For all of this to be happening to me, I must have done something wrong in God's eyes and He is, therefore, punishing me."

Well, I'd like to take a contrary view.

If you ever feel like that, if you ever feel that life's challenges are getting you down, if you ever doubt your own self-worth, I'd like you to consider Mary, the mother of Jesus. Just think about her life.

First, as a young girl, an angel appears to her and tells her that she is favored by God.

Great!

However, she is then told that she is going to have a baby.

Not so great…because the poor girl then has to go home and tell her family what many might think is a made-up story about an angel appearing to her and telling her that she is pregnant…by the Holy Spirit!

Furthermore, she also has to tell all of this to the man she is engaged to. She has to tell him that she's pregnant but assure him that he shouldn't worry or feel betrayed because God is responsible!

You can't blame Joseph for initially being skeptical at best, and, perhaps, more realistically, downright disgusted with and disbelieving of Mary. It can't have been easy for him or for her.

Skip forward then to Mary in her third trimester of pregnancy. Of all the times that the Romans could choose to conduct a census, it had to be right when Mary was, as they say, "heavy with child," and she and Joseph had to travel to register for the census. Travel in itself could not have been easy. Whether Mary was riding on a donkey or travelling on foot, it must have been very uncomfortable for her.

Then, on top of that, on the return journey, Mary went into labor. There were no rooms available, and the only way that she could give birth in private was to go into a cowshed, a dirty cave, and give birth to her baby there.

What must have gone through her mind? Her initial reaction must have been one of despondency and despair. She must have blamed herself. Mary must have thought to herself, "How am I messing this up so badly? I am going to give birth to this very special child of God, and I can't even find a decent place to deliver the child. What is God going to think of me, giving birth in a dirty cowshed?"

She must have thought to herself, "If I am so favored by God, how come all of this is happening to me?"

And so her life went on. It was certainly not a charmed life. It included losing Jesus for three days on a return trip from Jerusalem. And then, of course, just think of how she must have felt as her son, Jesus, the holy one of God, was seized, flogged, and then ignominiously nailed to a tree to die just like a common criminal.

That's how badly things went for Mary. That was God's plan for her.

It seems to me that, very often, God sends the toughest times to those whom he greatly favors: to the holy ones, just as he did to Mary, and, if you think about it, just as he did to His own son, Jesus.

Travel Tip to Remember
Instead of feeling despondent and despairing when your life seems to be one bad thing after another, take consolation in the fact that you are in good company with Mary and Jesus, and take consolation in the fact that you, too, must be a very special person in the eyes of God.

Acts 4:19-20

Peter and John, however, said to them in reply, "Whether it is right in the sight of God for us to obey you rather than God, you be the judges. It is impossible for us not to speak about what we have seen and heard."

Chapter

23

A few years ago, I remember getting the news that one of our children, together with her husband and children, was moving back to Arizona from another state. I was so happy. I was ecstatic. I wanted to tell everyone. Even my business colleagues told me that it showed in my whole demeanor.

This got me thinking. Am I a hypocrite? If this sort of good news gets me so excited, why don't I feel the same intensity of excitement and enthusiasm about the Gospel, about the really important Good News: the news that Christ imparted to us about how to inherit eternal life?

I started to ask myself if, perhaps, I didn't really believe that the Gospel is good news. I reasoned that if I did, surely it would show through in the way I led my life and the way I would want to share that with other people.

The conclusion I came to was that perhaps, like many people, outside of the physical church building, I can sometimes be best described as a "closet Christian."

I don't feel compelled like Peter and John to spread the Good News. I could never say, as they did, "It is impossible for me not to speak" about Jesus our Messiah. Those early Christians certainly felt this sense of delight, conviction, excitement, and desire to spread the Good News.

So what has changed between then and now?

In my case, I believe that I, at least, have spent a good deal of my life seeing Christianity too much in terms of the "form" and not enough in terms of the "substance." Jesus was all about "substance": the way we must love the Father and the way that love must overflow to love of our neighbor irrespective of who they are. It is all about selflessness. For my part, I have probably concentrated more on the rules and regulations rather than on pursuing a mission of living my life in the way that Jesus taught us.

If each of us showed a little more enthusiasm for the Good News: if we each had a true sense of mission about letting others know about the Good News by the selfless way we think, the selfless way we speak, and the selfless way we act and treat other people, then Christianity would spread rapidly. It would be like a smile. It would be contagious.

I think that would be a very worthy goal for a great many Christians. Let's stop being "Closet Christians." We have to strive for "Contagious Christianity," where we positively infect our fellow man.

Travel Tips to Remember
Don't spend your life as a "Closet Christian." Come out! Create an atmosphere of "Contagious Christianity" around you by the way you live your life—by the way you treat your fellow man. Be infected by the Good News (the Gospel) so much so that your happiness and positivity is noticed by those around you.

"WAY to go!"

Peter J. Moriarty

Matthew 13:47-51

Again, the kingdom of heaven is like a net thrown into the sea, which collects fish of every kind. When it is full they haul it ashore and sit down to put what is good into buckets. What is bad they throw away. Thus it will be at the end of the age. The angels will go out and separate the wicked from the righteous and throw them into the fiery furnace, where there will be wailing and grinding of teeth.

Chapter

24

A few years ago, I watched a movie called *August Rush*. It was about a young boy who could hear music in all of the sounds around him. He could hear rhythm and beauty in the multiplicity of everyday sounds: in everything…the sound of the wind, the sound of a breaking twig, a tin can, the tap of a shoe.

I enjoyed the movie, and it made me start to think about the fact that there are people in the world with extraordinary abilities and talents—not just people like the boy in the movie who can hear the distinct sounds of music but also artists who can see a multiplicity of uniquely defined colors in objects that appear to be just one color to most of us.

This thought process then led me to think about the fact that we all see and hear things differently. We all have different talents. We all have different interpretations of the world around us. Just because I see things in one way does not necessarily mean that you see them in the same way. Yet I automatically expect you to. In fact, if you don't see things in the same way as me, I may be offended or upset or even afraid.

Unfortunately, that's the way we tend to be as human beings. If people living in our own country cannot see and agree on things in the same way, just think how difficult it is for people living in different countries and brought-up with different cultural perspectives to agree with us and our points of view. We all see things in different ways, and just because someone doesn't see things in the same way as us, certainly that doesn't necessarily mean that they are wrong.

For many of us, we think that our way is the right way or, very often, the only way, yet we hear in the New Testament how "The Kingdom of Heaven is like a net thrown into the sea, which collects fish of every kind."

"Fish of every kind." That's us. God created each and every one of us, and He also created our differences. We should rejoice in those differences, but often, we do not.

Jesus preached a gospel of tolerance and understanding. Yet intolerance is one of the biggest issues in the world today. It can even start in our homes, in our families, in our communities, and in our places of work.

At some time, perhaps even on most days, it is probable that many of us will get annoyed with someone else. It is often because they do not see things in the same way as we do. We automatically jump to the conclusion that the other person must be wrong. But that might very well be a wrong conclusion. It is possible that they just see things in a different way. That doesn't necessarily mean that they are incorrect.

When we read in the Gospel about God casting His net and collecting fish of many kinds, this should remind us that Jesus wants us to understand and accept that God made us with differences. We, therefore, need to make an extra effort to be more understanding of people's differences.

We need to be more tolerant. We each have different types of gifts and ways of understanding: different ways of interpreting what we hear and different ways of translating what we see, just as the boy did in *August Rush*.

Travel Tip to Remember
Everyone has goodness in them. It's our job as followers of Jesus Christ to try to discover that goodness in our fellow man, no matter how deeply that goodness might seem to be hidden to our eyes. Remember, your fellow man might just see things in a different way, but that doesn't make them wrong.

Peter J. Moriarty

Matthew 6:9-13

"This is how you are to pray:
Our Father in heaven, hallowed be your name,
your kingdom come, your will be done,
on earth as in heaven.
Give us today our daily bread;
and forgive us our debts,
as we forgive our debtors;
and do not subject us to the final test,
but deliver us from the evil one."

Chapter

25

I want to share a couple of pieces of my dirty laundry: Christian dirty laundry, that is.

I am frightened of dying.

I don't think that I am alone in that fear, but it begs the question, "Where have I gone wrong?" I must have gone wrong because, as a practicing Christian, I have spent my whole life claiming to believe in God and the reward of eternal life.

Am I a hypocrite? Do I really believe that from the beginning of time God always intended to come among us, in the form of Jesus Christ, to show us, through his words and his example, how to lead our lives in such a way that we may have eternal life after we die?

Do I believe this or am I just playing at being a Christian?

Clearly, I need to start to see death as the essential step forward to a life of everlasting happiness.

This reminds me of another piece of dirty laundry with which I struggle.

For a great deal of my life, I always said formalized prayers that I had been taught as a child or prayed to a saint for help. I did not speak to God directly as I do now. Also, I would often barter with the saints for the granting of some special favor, and yet in the New Testament, Jesus told us quite clearly that we should pray directly to the Father—and that we don't have to barter. God already knows our needs, and like any loving Father, He will give us what we need (provided, of course, that it is good for us).

As I have matured as a Christian, I have realized that I have to accept Jesus at his word and see death as the natural and necessary gateway to our eternal home in Heaven. If I don't accept Jesus at his word, I can expect a similar response to the one that Jesus gave to the Jews who gathered around him in the temple area. The Jews said to Jesus, "Tell us plainly, are you or are you not the Messiah." Jesus replied something to the effect of, "I keep telling you and showing you that I am, but you still don't take any notice of me."

Two thousand years later, many of us still seem to ignore the way Jesus taught us to pray, and two thousand years later, many of us are still very fearful of dying. It may not be intentional, but it's almost as though we really do not believe what Jesus taught us.

The gospels teach us that "life is about dying and rising." The gospels help us to more fully appreciate the inevitability of our deaths. They help us to see death as the welcome transition point to the achievement of eternal life: the life of peace and happiness that awaits each of us that seek it, just as God intended it to be.

Travel Tip to Remember

Focus on talking to God. Talk to Him as you would to a loving father. Have absolute confidence that God, your father, only wants the best for you. He knows what you need, but just like a loving father, He does not object to hearing you ask for it but will not grant something that He knows is bad for you.

Also remember that when bad things happen, they often happen for a good reason and good things come of them.

Peter J. Moriarty

Luke 4:16-24, 28-30

He came to Nazareth, where he had grown up, and went according to his custom into the synagogue on the sabbath day. He stood up to read and was handed a scroll of the prophet Isaiah. He unrolled the scroll and found the passage where it was written: "The Spirit of the Lord is upon me, because he has anointed me to bring glad tidings to the poor. He has sent me to proclaim liberty to captives and recovery of sight to the blind, to let the oppressed go free and to proclaim a year acceptable to the Lord." Rolling up the scroll, he handed it back to the attendant and sat down, and the eyes of all in the synagogue looked intently at him. He said to them, "Today this scripture passage is fulfilled in your hearing." And all spoke highly of him and were amazed at the gracious words that came from his mouth. They also asked, "Isn't this the son of Joseph?" He said to them, "Surely you will quote me this proverb, 'Physician, cure yourself,' and say, 'Do here in your native place the things that we heard were done in Capernaum.'" And he said, "Amen, I say to you, no prophet is accepted in his own native place."

When the people in the synagogue heard this, they were all filled with fury. They rose up, drove him out of the town, and led him to the brow of the hill on which their town had been built, to hurl him down headlong. But he passed through the midst of them and went away.

Chapter

26

I knew a school teacher at the local high school. I was very close to him and his parents, who were lovely, down-to-earth people—what we would also refer to in England as "salt of the earth."

This high school teacher met a girl from Australia. They got married, had a few children, and then the school teacher, and not his wife, got the urge to move to Australia. So off they went to Australia, and the high school teacher became a high school principal in Australia.

The next thing I heard was that he had earned his Ph.D. in psychology and was writing best-selling books on the subject—books that were then used as college reference materials. Then I heard that he had psychology clinics all over Australia, as well as radio and television shows. This was in addition to owning restaurants and hotels.

Unfortunately, I didn't stay in touch with him as much as I should have done while he was making these great strides in Australia. It's no excuse, but during that same time period, my wife, our three children, and I moved first from England to Kenya, then to Denmark, and then to Norway before being moved again by my company to the corporate headquarters in New Jersey, USA.

Shortly after arriving in New Jersey, I was contacted by this person in Australia who wanted to come to stay with us. By this time, he had started another successful business as a consultant to politicians. Apparently, his particular area of expertise was the art of "negotiating." He taught these skills not just to Australian politicians but also to politicians in the United States. However, he told me that on this occasion, the primary reason for his visit was to appear before the United Nations Assembly regarding negotiations with a certain country, and he had also agreed to be interviewed by some American television stations while he was here.

I was amazed—actually astounded—and deep down, I was possibly a bit jealous. I think I resented this person's "makeover." I probably thought to myself, "Who does he think he is? I know him. He was just an ordinary school teacher from an ordinary industrial city in England, brought-up by an ordinary, down-to-earth family. He surely can't be this revered person—this "guru" getting all of this international attention."

It occurred to me that I was acting in the same way as the family, friends, and acquaintances of Jesus when he made the visit to Nazareth during his ministry. You will recall that the people who lived in his own home town, and heard him speak in the synagogue, were so incensed with Jesus that they wanted to throw him off a cliff.

I was reacting in just the same way. I knew this person's mother and father. They were ordinary people. I knew his brother. I had a real hard time believing that this person who was now staying with our family in New Jersey was really the person that he was now perceived to be.

When I step back and think about it, I think that, possibly, this person always had a deep yearning inside to be something different. I think that he knew that he had the ability to be much more than he was. He probably had that burning desire to use all of his talents—a desire to recreate himself.

I believe that a great many of us have a desire to recreate ourselves spiritually: to be much more committed to God than we currently are. I believe that deep inside, we all know that we can be better. It doesn't have to be something big, but it is often something that requires an act of bravery because we are all afraid of what others will think or say if we change ourselves into the person that we always wanted to be.

Sometimes, people have to go away to another city, state, or country in order to recreate themselves, just as this person did. Sometimes people just "bite the bullet" or "take the bull by the horns" and make the changes in their lives that they know they need to make in order to achieve their goal of being everything that they know they can be. On the other hand, some are just too scared of what others may say or think.

Perhaps today is the day for you to really have courage and make a firm resolution to be the son or daughter of God that you know you want to be, without fear of what your friends or family will say.

Travel Tip to Remember
We all have the ability to be much more than we are. Deep inside, we all know that we can be better. Seek out that

desire to recreate yourself spiritually. You don't have to do something big, but it might be something that requires an act of bravery—bravery because most of us are afraid of what others may think or say if we change ourselves into the person that we always wanted to be. Be brave. Take that first step towards recreating yourself spiritually.

"WAY to go!"

Peter J. Moriarty

Acts 14:8-12

*At Lystra there was a crippled man, lame from birth, who
had never walked. He listened to Paul speaking, who
looked intently at him, saw that he had the faith to be
healed, and called out in a loud voice, "Stand up straight
on your feet." He jumped up and began to walk
about. [11] When the crowds saw what Paul had done, they
cried out in Lycaonian, "The gods have come down to us
in human form." They called Barnabas "Zeus" and Paul
"Hermes," because he was the chief speaker.*

Chapter

27

Some time ago, I was on a business trip that took me first to Chicago, then to New York, and then to Boston. From Boston, I drove to a small beach town in Maine and then back to Boston, eventually returning to Phoenix. It was quite a trip…in many ways.

While in Maine, I attended a meeting with the senior management team of another company, during which I was asked to address the group concerning my perspectives on what was happening in the pharmaceutical industry and my vision for the future of that industry.

The small audience seemed to be extremely impressed by my apparent insights and by my vision of what needed to happen in the future to correct some of the challenges that the industry was facing.

Following my address, it seemed as though those who had attended really thought that I was some sort of guru, blessed with special powers that allowed me to see clearly what was happening, what was going to happen, and what actions needed to be taken by their company.

It was one of those experiences where there is a terrible tendency to get filled with self-important thoughts. People start to treat you in a special way, and you start to believe that you are "something special."

That's when the warning signals need to go off. That's when your head begins to swell with thoughts of how great you are. Thoughts of "I am something special."

Unfortunately for many of us, we have a tendency to revel in this. We start to believe the excessive praises of others, no matter who we are or what we have achieved or, perhaps, not even achieved. The tendency is the same. We really start to think we are "great." Our egos get on top of us, and we think that we can do it all by ourselves—that we have extraordinary talents—that we are different and better than other people. We feel as though we have become almost gods among the people.

Those large egos lead to large degrees of selfishness and feelings of self-importance. These are great danger signals.

In the New Testament, we read in Acts that that is what could have happened to Paul and Barnabas. The people were so impressed by the miracle that Paul and Barnabas had performed that the people viewed them as Gods and wanted to treat them accordingly.

It would have been only too easy for Paul and Barnabas to have gone along with this just for a little while. All of us have a tendency to wallow in a bit of "hero worship," but that is the slippery road to self-destruction. Once we begin to think that we are God-like, even in small ways, we are then easily tempted to trust in ourselves. We start to shut out God or at least forget about Him for a while. We start to believe that we can do it all on our own—that we do not need God.

The reality is that we all need God. We cannot do it on our own. We need to constantly remind ourselves that those talents that we have come from God. They are not of our own making. If we do not stop these desires to be worshipped as soon as they start to arise, then it is only going to get harder to resist the temptation. There is a tremendous desire in many of us to want to be the center of attention. We want other people to notice us. We are only too willing to let our egos roam unchecked. This is when we start to move away from our reliance on God.

We all need to keep our egos in check. We need to be meticulous about not letting the praises of others lead us to think that we are something special. We need to continuously acknowledge the presence of God in everything that we do: realizing that we cannot do anything without Him. We need to be mindful that every talent and ability that we have are gifts from God and that God expects us to use them optimally, maximally, and selflessly. God also expects us to work diligently to play our part in continually improving those talents and abilities. However, we should always remember that they are gifts from God. We must not let our egos get the better of us by thinking, even in the slightest way, that we are "God's gift to the world," as the saying goes.

Travel Tip to Remember
Look out for the danger signals. When the world starts to praise you, put your ego in check. Never let your mind be filled with thoughts of your own self-importance. Remember that your abilities and talents are gifts from God. Your duty is to use them optimally, maximally, and perhaps most of all, selflessly.

Mark 8:34-35

He summoned the crowd with his disciples and said to them, "Whoever wishes to come after me must deny himself, take up his cross, and follow me. For whoever wishes to save his life will lose it, but whoever loses his life for my sake and that of the gospel will save it."

Exodus 14:21-22

Then Moses stretched out his hand over the sea; and the Lord drove back the sea with a strong east wind all night long and turned the sea into dry ground. The waters were split, so that the Israelites entered into the midst of the sea on dry land, with the water as a wall to their right and to their left.

Chapter

28

Some years ago, I was visiting England on a business trip when I bumped into an old friend of mine. When I had last seen him, he was the managing director of an advertising agency. He was a typical advertising agency executive: he ate too much, drank too much, and was always focused on fun, especially when entertaining his agency's clients. His life seemed to revolve around the agency, and he certainly gave no impression of having God in his life.

However, the man I met that morning in England was not the same person. He was now clearly a committed Christian who was obviously extremely caring and considerate of his fellow man. I subsequently came to hear from his wife about the events that had brought about his conversion to becoming a seriously committed Christian. The events were as follows:

His wife was a very devoted Christian, and an active member of her church community. She attended church frequently and not just on Sundays. She had been trying for years to get her husband to attend church services, but he would not. She tried all of the conventional ways that she thought would entice him, but he was just not interested. Then she decided to offer it all up to God and asked God what she should do.

In her words, she felt that she got a very strange response from God. She said that she felt that God was telling her not to go to Church so much: to spend more time with her husband. So she started to do just that. She spent more time with her husband. It seemed to have such a noticeable effect on him that one day he decided he would accompany her to one of the church services. However, my friend subsequently told me that he did that just to keep his wife happy, and not because he was in any way interested in religion. As it turned out, he did it two or three times to make his wife happy. Then one day, the minister asked if anyone in the congregation wanted to give themselves to Christ. As I was told by my friend, "It was the strangest thing. I got up and walked to the front of the Church…and the rest is history."

Sometime later, I asked my friend about how his life as a Christian was progressing. He said that he had to re-educate himself. He was trying to exert some real self-discipline. Instead of just getting everything and anything he wanted, as in the past, he was now self-imposing fasts and abstinence from alcohol for some periods each month.

When I think back on this, it makes me realize that if we do not self-impose some sacrifices, it becomes more and more difficult for us to resist temptation. That is one of the benefits of self-imposed fasting and abstaining from certain things.

I went on to have a long and successful business relationship with this friend but also benefited greatly by three key things that this relationship taught me:

a) Never give up on someone just because they are currently not of the same religious beliefs as you, even if they have no apparent beliefs. Particularly, don't give up on any family members who are apparently no longer following your religion's practices.

b) Always trust in God to show you the way, and accept that God's way may be unconventional and certainly not the way that you might have expected or chosen.

c) And last, but certainly not least, Christianity is a serious business. It takes some working on, including imposing regular self-discipline such as giving up things we really like for some period of time.

The New Testament tells us that we have to be prepared to make (self) sacrifices, to take up our cross, in the pursuit of the Kingdom of Heaven. Spreading the Good News of salvation is even more important than family. Christianity is a serious business. We have to be prepared to give up things that we want to do. Seeking the Kingdom of God is paramount.

Finally, just look at what God told Moses to do: lead his people into the Red Sea. That must have been frightening. Yet God parted the sea and enabled the Israelites to escape the Egyptians. God's way was unconventional, just as it seemed very unconventional for my friend's wife to go to church less in order to win her husband over for Christ.

Travel Tip to Remember
Clearly, with God, everything is possible, no matter how impossible a circumstance or situation may seem to you. It

is that belief, confidence, and trust in God that is so important to our successful travel along the pathway to Heaven. So ask yourself the following question and answer yourself honestly: "Do I currently have enough confidence in God to trust in Him and to entrust all things to Him?"

"WAY to go!"

1 John 4:11-12

Beloved, if God so loved us, we also must love one another. No one has ever seen God. Yet, if we love one another, God remains in us, and his love is brought to perfection in us.

Romans 5:8

But God proves his love for us in that while we were still sinners Christ died for us.

Chapter

29

Some time ago, a friend recommended a book entitled *Happiness Now*, written by Robert Holden, Ph.D. One particular passage in the book really struck me. Holden, a psychologist, was being visited in his clinic by Paul, a self-made millionaire. Paul told Holden that he had three children and that he wanted to give them everything. He said that he loved them more than anything. He went on to say that he wanted to give them everything that he didn't have when he was growing up. He also added that he was constantly telling them that they could be whatever they want to be.

As related in Holden's book, Paul then went on to say that he encourages his children to work really hard, to make every effort to be the best that they can be. He said that he always reminds them that they can do better, that they can give more, and that they can be more—that there are no limits.

Paul had gone on about this for some time when Holden stopped him and asked the following question: "What is it that you are really trying to tell me, Paul?"

Paul bowed his head and said, "The trouble is my children hate me. I've given them everything, and they hate me."

Following this, Holden went on to say that he asked Paul if he ever told his children how wonderful they are *right now*. He inquired if he told the children that he loved them *just as they are.* Holden told Paul that children don't need to be told how great they are going to be. What they need to be told is how loved and how wonderful they are now, and, he added, by telling the children how wonderful he thinks they are now, Paul would be investing wisely in their future.

Paul answered in the negative. He never spoke to his children in that way.

The point that Robert Holden was making was that we need to let our children know that they are loved just as they are, without having to prove themselves or be something different—that we love them for who they are—that we love them unreservedly, without any strings attached.

On putting down the book, it occurred to me that what Robert Holden was advising was that we must simply love in the way that our Heavenly Father loves us. God loves us unconditionally as we are, even if we feel that we are the greatest sinners that have ever walked this earth.

Thinking of us as "big sinners" is perhaps one of the greatest challenges that many Christians face. This is because, for many of us, a negative side-effect of our religious upbringing is that we think only in terms of avoiding sin. We think of being or doing something different in order to avoid the punishment that we believe such sin will attract. That really does not make sense if we really understand and appreciate God's love for us.

Think about it. God loves us exactly as we are, even in our state of sinfulness. That is very comforting. It certainly makes me realize that I can really feel very close to God because God accepts me totally, irrespective of my faults. His love is unconditional. Once I start to think of God in those terms—once I stop thinking that God is only interested in what I could be like in the future—then I can start to love Him properly and more fully. I can stop worrying about avoiding sin. Then, just like the children referenced in Holden's book, I can start to focus on returning the love that is poured out by the parent, God, our Father. Then I will want to do things to please the Father. I will not be so concerned about avoiding sin but be more concerned about how much I can love. That, in it, will lead me to make the right decisions that reflect my love of the Father.

Travel Tip to Remember
Really think about the fact that God loves us as we are. As with any parent, God wants the best for us. Nevertheless, he loves us absolutely and unconditionally, even in our present sinfulness. If this becomes your mindset, you will want to be the best you can be because you don't want to let God down; instead, you will want to be as like Him as you can possibly be.

Peter J. Moriarty

John 1:1-5

In the beginning was the Word,
and the Word was with God,
and the Word was God.
He was in the beginning with God.
All things came to be through him,
and without him nothing came to be.
What came to be through him was life,
and this life was the light of the human race;
the light shines in the darkness,
and the darkness has not overcome it.

Chapter

30

A few years ago, I saw two television movies about Pope John Paul II. There were three distinct things that struck me about these movies.

The first was how positively uplifted and inspired I felt by watching them. Both movies had a very positive impact on me. They made me feel that I wanted to lead a better life. They made me feel that I wanted to be more loving and caring towards other people. They made me feel as though I wanted to share more with others.

The second was the realization that most other television programs can have a largely negative impact on us. We are constantly bombarded by programs that portray success in life as one where you get ahead at the expense of others— where greed and selfishness are the norm and an acceptable way to lead our lives.

The third thing that impacted me was a scene in one of the movies where the Pope is talking to a woman who is racked with guilt over her sins. The Pope turns to her and says, "Always remember that God judges us by how much we love, and not by how much we sin."

When I heard that, I thought, "Wow! If only this was the way that we all learned about God and our relationship with Him. What a more powerful force Christianity would be in the world."

Instead, most of us have grown-up being taught that Christianity is all about avoiding sin. We have this image of God as the great judge in the sky who is constantly looking down on us to see when we commit sins: a God who is always condemning us to some form of punishment for each and every one of our transgressions.

This is such an incorrect image of God.

God is foremost a God of love. A God of unconditional love. A God that wants us to love Him and our fellow man in the same way.

Our vision or image of God must start with grace, light, and love rather than sin, darkness, and punishment. From the beginning of time, God, in His absolute unconditional love for us, intended to give Himself to us. God always intended to come among us in human form, in the person of Jesus the Christ, to teach us, by word and example, how to love Him and our fellow man.

God did this not because something had gone terribly wrong with His plan for mankind when we sinned in the Garden of Eden. He did not conclude that because we had sinned He had to send in Jesus to die for our sins. God always intended to come among us. He always intended to come to teach us. He always intended to come and show us by His example how we should lead our lives by loving Him and loving our neighbors, the rest of mankind, without exceptions. He showed us that we are to love our fellow man no matter the color of their skin, their language, appearance or position in life. Jesus said that these were the two most important commandments: love the Lord your God with your whole heart, your whole soul, your whole mind, and (love) your neighbor as yourself.

God, through His son, Jesus, clearly taught us that we must focus on learning to love Him and on increasing our love for our fellow man. This is the exact opposite of just trying to avoid sin, as many of us have been doing for most of our lives.

Many of us are somehow trapped in the "sin complex," out of which we clearly need to escape and free ourselves to focus on loving God and our fellow man.

But let me make this perfectly clear: I am not advocating that we should sin. What I am advocating is that we should increase our love by practicing acts of kindness, generosity, and selflessness, rather than just focusing on avoiding sin.

It seems to me that if we love more, we will sin less.

Just think about it. Most, if not all, sins generally stem from our own selfishness. We put our own self-interests before God and our fellow man. This concept of focusing on loving more rather than focusing on trying to avoid sin is not rocket science. It seems to be logical. When I think about my own family life, it seems to give further credence to the concept, and helps me to more completely understand that God judges us more by how much we love rather than by how much we sin. This is because I love my wife and my children with all my heart. As a result, I try to lead my life in such a way that I do not do anything to hurt them or offend them. It starts with my love for them and my consequent desire to do good things for them in order to please them and make them happy. I act in this way out of love, not because I am frightened of being punished by them.

Surely, this is how we should act with regard to God.

Travel Tip to Remember
Our path to Heaven must start from the basis of love and not from the basis of fear. We need to change our focus from avoiding sin to loving more because if we love more, we will sin less.

"WAY to go!"

John 21:15-17

When they had finished breakfast, Jesus said to Simon Peter, "Simon, son of John, do you love me more than these?" He said to him, "Yes, Lord, you know that I love you." He said to him, "Feed my lambs." He then said to him a second time, "Simon, son of John, do you love me?" He said to him, "Yes, Lord, you know that I love you." He said to him, "Tend my sheep." He said to him the third time, "Simon, son of John, do you love me?" Peter was distressed that he had said to him a third time, "Do you love me?" and he said to him, "Lord, you know everything; you know that I love you." [Jesus] said to him, "Feed my sheep."

Chapter

31

As a child, I really did not like reading. I can remember hearing my parents saying to me, "Peter, why don't you sit down and read a book like your sisters instead of messing around?" And I can imagine my reply: "Because I'd rather just mess around, and they are just goody-goodies." Now that I'm older, I really do enjoy reading.

If we were to take a national poll about reading habits, I am sure that a very large portion of the male population, and probably quite a lot of the female population as well, would admit that when they do read, it is predominantly about sports.

I think that the reality is that we all tend to want to read as much as we can about whatever is at the center of our lives. In the case of many people, it is sports. We all want to keep up on the subjects that we really enjoy. We want to be able to converse with others about it and have an educated opinion—a point of view that is seen as being up to date. We like to have the facts, and in the case of sports, we very often must have the latest statistics. We want to be so knowledgeable in that area that others are going to want to listen to us.

If you sit back and reflect on this, perhaps something has gone wrong with the priorities of the majority of the population. God is meant to be the center of our lives. Why is it, therefore, that the majority of Christians do not bother to read about or educate themselves on a continuous basis about matters related to God and to spirituality?

I suspect that if we were to take a poll in most Christian churches on a Sunday, the overwhelming majority of the people attending would have to admit to never having read a book in recent years, specifically about God, their religion, or about any form of spirituality. Yet if the same group of people were to be asked when they last read anything about sports, the vast majority would have to admit that they have done so very recently.

Why does God, apparently, mean so little to most of us? Why don't most of us feel a commitment to read, to study, to listen, to learn, to educate ourselves and hone our skills and knowledge about the very subject, the very person, who is meant to be the center of our lives?

When we read in the gospel of Christ's exhortation to Peter, "Feed my lambs....Feed my sheep," this is not a passive instruction for the rest of us to just sit back and be fed by the religious leaders of the church. As the saying goes, "You can take a horse to water, but you can't make it drink," and it is just so with us. We can be offered the food to help develop our knowledge and appreciation of God and his son Jesus Christ, but we have got to be willing to accept this food to nourish our spiritual development. If we don't deliberately make an effort to continually educate ourselves about our Christian religion, then we are no better than sheep.

The gospels exhort us not to be just like sheep, blindly following, but to be sheep that are hungry to be fed by

God, the center of our lives, about whom we want to learn more and more.

I think our constant prayer as Christians has to be that the church will come alive with people whose lives are centered around God—people who are interested in educating themselves about God and their relationship with Him—people who are at least as much, and ideally more, interested in reading and learning about God as they are interested in reading and learning about the latest sports results and statistics.

Travel Tip to Remember
Strive to continually educate yourselves about our Christian religion. Consider being as well informed about it as you are about sports or whatever else your passion is in life.

Peter J. Moriarty

John 20:11-18

*Mary stayed outside the tomb weeping. And as she wept,
she bent over into the tomb and saw two angels in white
sitting there, one at the head and one at the feet where the
body of Jesus had been. And they said to her, "Woman,
why are you weeping?" She said to them, "They have
taken my Lord, and I don't know where they laid him."
When she had said this, she turned around and saw Jesus
there, but did not know it was Jesus. Jesus said to her,
"Woman, why are you weeping? Whom are you looking
for?" She thought it was the gardener and said to him,
"Sir, if you carried him away, tell me where you laid him,
and I will take him." Jesus said to her, "Mary!" She
turned and said to him in Hebrew, "Rabbouni," which
means Teacher. Jesus said to her, "Stop holding on to me,
for I have not yet ascended to the Father. But go to my
brothers and tell them, 'I am going to my Father and your
Father, to my God and your God.'" Mary of Magdala
went and announced to the disciples, "I have seen the
Lord," and what he told her.*

Chapter

32

Have you ever been guilty of pre-judging a person before you have even spoken to them? Do your preconceived ideas about someone ever turn out to be completely incorrect? I have certainly been guilty of this on many occasions.

For example, I remember many years ago when I was living in Norway, most mornings I would see a Norwegian gentleman walking to his office, which was in the same building as my own office. I am sure that I must have looked at him many times and thought to myself, "Well, there is someone who leads a very uneventful, perhaps even boring life and has probably never done anything exciting or out of the ordinary." I had come to that conclusion without ever having a conversation with him. In fact, the most contact I'd had with him was the morning nod of the head and a quick "god morgen" ("good morning").

Then one day we did actually stop and have a conversation. He had a great command of English. We talked for a short while, and then he invited me to his office. Once I was in his office and we carried on our conversation, I learned that the person I had assumed had led a boring life was, in reality, one of the most famous spies in World War II. He was so famous that the British Television Corporation, the BBC, had just made a documentary about him and his wartime partner spy. They were known in the war by the code name "Mutt and Jeff."

They were, in fact, double agents, who worked with the British to deceive the Nazis.

It was a long and fascinating story but one that ended with the man who was now sitting across the table from me relating how he had been imprisoned at one point, accused of actually being a spy for the Germans. It was quite some time after the end of the war before the British publicly acknowledged that he and his partner were, in fact, double agents, acting on behalf of the British government.

He was far from the boring clerk that I had imagined. I had judged him even before I had really spoken to him, and I was wrong.

This incident recently came to mind when I was reading the gospel about how, three days after the death of Jesus, Mary Magdalene found the empty tomb. While she was there, full of sorrow and confusion because someone seemed to have stolen the body of Jesus, she saw a man she assumed to be the gardener. It was only when she spoke with him that she realized that it was Jesus.

How often do we fail to talk to someone because of preconceived ideas of who they are or where they are from? How often do we shun contact with an individual because we feel that we will have nothing in common or, even worse, because they are not "our type of people"? I know that I have been guilty of that on many occasions, and I suspect that most people have been at some stage in their lives.

It is often only by taking the trouble to talk to someone, to communicate with them, that we can have the opportunity to hear and see Jesus shining through them.

That is what the gospel story of Mary Magdalene should remind us about—that we must make time for our fellow man—That we must reach out to others, to show our love for our fellow man, no matter who they are, where they are from, or what they have done. We must always be mindful that everyone has Jesus in them.

Sometimes, the fact that everyone has Jesus in them may seem to be well hidden, but it is there if we only take the trouble to find it.

For my part, I know I need to stop pre-judging people. I need to extend a welcoming smile and a welcoming word to everyone with whom I come into contact. I know I must be a reflection of the risen Lord—the welcoming voice, the outstretched hand, the caring and consoling word.

The risen Jesus is ever present in each and every person. It's up to us to discover him.

Travel Tip to Remember
Make a point of striving to never pre-judge people. Instead, give everyone a chance. Take the time to hear their story.

John 1:29-31

The next day he saw Jesus coming toward him and said, "Behold, the Lamb of God, who takes away the sin of the world. He is the one of whom I said, 'A man is coming after me who ranks ahead of me because he existed before me.' I did not know him, but the reason why I came baptizing with water was that he might be made known to Israel."

Chapter

33

Do you ever wake up in the middle of the night and start worrying? Worrying about how things are going wrong and not to plan?

I certainly find that things are so much worse in the night when it's dark. I, therefore, deliberately try to remind myself that it will all seem so much better in the morning and also that what I think of as my plan is not always in line with the plan that God has for me.

One of my sons related to me a dream that he had. He dreamed that he and two of his friends were rushing to catch a train. One of his friends got on the train, but my son and his other friend missed it. Apparently, it was the only train going where my son and his friends had planned to go.

As a result, my son ended up catching another train that was not going in the same direction, and he was very disappointed. However, some way into the journey, my son found out that this train was going to Heaven. He described to me how incredible he felt when he found out. He said that there was joy and relief because he found out that he was definitely going to Heaven.

Sometimes, what we plan for is not what God plans for us. We need to trust in God, particularly when we are going through our most difficult times: when we are disappointed or even despondent. We should not be afraid. God is always with us. Sometimes we just don't listen enough to God. We don't let him reveal himself to us. At least, I know I don't.

In one of the gospels, we hear of the encounter between John the Baptist and Jesus. Do you think that John always knew what he was eventually being called to do? Do you think that he always knew that he was to be the one who prepared the way for the coming of the Messiah? Do you think that Jesus always knew that he was the Son of God?

I believe that these were almost certainly gradual revelations. I think His Father's plan for him gradually unfolded.

Jesus was, of course, the supreme example of openness and trust in God. It was not Jesus' plan that was important to him. It was the plan that God, his Father, gradually revealed to him that guided Jesus' life. We need to do the same. We need to be open to and trust in God and the plan that He has for us.

I believe that most of us would like to believe that we would always say "yes" to God's calling. However, we cannot do that unless we are honestly open to listening to God's gradual revelation of His plan for us.

Travel Tip to Remember
Learn to let God's particular plan for you be revealed. Appreciate that God's timescale is not always the same as our chronological approach to time. Trust in God at all times because He knows what is best for you, and

remember this particularly during your darkest and most difficult and challenging times.

1 Samuel 24:3-12

*So Saul took three thousand of the best men from all Israel
and went in search of David and his men in the direction
of the wild goat crags. When he came to the sheepfolds
along the way, he found a cave, which he entered to relieve
himself. David and his men were occupying the inmost
recesses of the cave. David's servants said to him, "This is
the day about which the Lord said to you: I will deliver
your enemy into your hand; do with him as you see fit." So
David moved up and stealthily cut off an end of Saul's
robe. Afterward, however, David regretted that he had cut
off an end of Saul's robe. He said to his men, "The Lord
forbid that I should do such a thing to my master,
the Lord's anointed, to lay a hand on him, for he is
the Lord's anointed." With these words David restrained
his men and would not permit them to attack Saul. Saul
then left the cave and went on his way. David also stepped
out of the cave, calling to Saul, "My lord the king!" When
Saul looked back, David bowed, his face to the ground in
homage, and asked Saul: "Why do you listen to those who
say, 'David is trying to harm you'? You see for yourself
today that the Lord just now delivered you into my hand in
the cave. I was told to kill you, but I took pity on you
instead. I decided, 'I will not raise a hand against my
master, for he is the Lord's anointed.' Look here, my
father. See the end of your robe which I hold. I cut off an
end of your robe and did not kill you. Now see and be
convinced that I plan no harm and no rebellion. I have
done you no wrong, though you are hunting me down to
take my life.'*

Chapter

34

Some years ago, a visiting priest conducted the Sunday service at the church I attend. I particularly remember a comment he made about holding grudges. He said that if you hold a grudge or are angry and resentful of another person, it's like taking poison yourself in the hopes that you will kill the other person.

I believe the opposite is also true.

If you are a kind and generous person: if you smile, lend a helping hand, reach out and make the first move to forgive someone even when you are absolutely sure that you are in the right and the other person has done you wrong, you create a "double whammy." The other person feels better but so do you.

As a result of this priest's comments and my subsequent thoughts about creating a "double whammy," I decided to try a little experiment.

At that time, I had moved my company into a new office building. Initially, of course, I did not know many people in the other companies occupying the building. However, I did pass a lot of people each day in the corridor. So each time I saw someone coming my way, particularly if they looked glum and miserable, I would try to make eye contact with them, smile, and say, "Good morning" or "Hi. How are you?"

When I did this, I was constantly astounded by how the faces of those people lit up and broke out into a smile. Miserable-looking faces suddenly became pictures of happiness just because someone that they didn't know took the trouble to smile at them and greet them. It seemed to work wonders for so many of them, and it certainly worked a little miracle for me.

In the Old Testament, we read of the complete act of generosity and kindness extended by David to Saul. Saul was very much against David. In fact, David feared for his life from Saul. Yet it was David who extended the hand of friendship. It was David who was the first to set aside old grudges when he found Saul in a very vulnerable position. Even though Saul was out to get David, David did not kill Saul while he slept, and he certainly had the opportunity to do just that. Instead, he merely cut off a piece of Saul's clothing. He just wanted to show Saul that he had been close enough to have killed him and that what he wanted was not Saul's death but reconciliation with him. And the reconciliation did occur. The results were probably even better than David could have expected.

We read in the Gospels of how Jesus selected and named his apostles, those he chose to go out and spread His message of love and forgiveness. In fact, the word "apostle" means a "personal messenger" or "a person who is commissioned or charged with transmitting the message." We too are called to spread that simple message. That is our "calling." We should be the first to offer the hand of reconciliation in an argument. We are called to be the person who looks a stranger in the eye and offers a smile: the one who goes out of their way to make someone feel comfortable in an uncomfortable situation.

These are simple ways of starting to spread the message of the Gospel. This is how we can start to show love for our neighbor, for our fellow man, and it also has the "double whammy" of making us feel really good.

Travel Tip to Remember
Don't hold grudges. It's like taking poison yourself in the hope of killing the person you hold the grudge against. Preach the Gospel by the way you live your life. As St. Francis of Assisi is reputed to have said, "Preach the Gospel at all times. Use words if necessary."

Peter J. Moriarty

Acts 4:32-35

*The community of believers was of one heart and mind,
and no one claimed that any of his possessions was his
own, but they had everything in common. With great power
the apostles bore witness to the resurrection of the Lord
Jesus, and great favor was accorded them all. There was
no needy person among them, for those who owned
property or houses would sell them, bring the proceeds of
the sale, and put them at the feet of the apostles, and they
were distributed to each according to need.*

Chapter

35

I have a problem. At least my wife says I do. The problem is that I can't keep my mouth shut. There are certain situations that arise where I just seem to be compelled to say something. For example, if I see total inefficiencies in shops or businesses, I can't seem to help myself from passing a comment. If someone is discourteous, I seem to be able to almost automatically open my mouth and criticize them—obviously being somewhat discourteous myself.

It's almost as if I am compelled to do it, and my wife often just tells me to "zip it." She says she can see it on my face or in my body language when she knows that I am going to open this big mouth of mine.

I claim it's a compulsion—which is basically an admission of a lack of self-control on my part. That's bad enough, but I think that the reality is that it is more like a habit. I think that many of us have habits like this. We sometimes just feel compelled to say something back to someone: sometimes in retaliation, sometimes in frustration, and sometimes we say things without thinking. We comment on their incompetence or perhaps, even worse, we say things behind peoples' backs. We "tittle tattle" to others about them and, often times, what we say is not very complimentary.

Now, my mother-in-law was exactly the opposite. She used to say, "If you haven't got anything good to say about someone, don't bother saying anything at all."

I think that's a great principle. It's one that I keep trying to adopt. I also think that it is an intrinsically Christian principle.

Just try it even for one day. It's hard to keep. At least I find it hard, and it makes me realize just how often I actually do say non-complimentary things about other people.

You might want to try it for yourself because, if you think about it, we are all called to be examples to those around us. Paul and the early Christians were known by the way they treated one another and those around them. They came across as people filled with something special: the Holy Spirit, the Paraclete, the Advocate. People were attracted to Christianity by the way the Christians acted—and reacted—by the things they said and the things they did. And I believe that today, the way that we treat one another, including those people we don't even know, can have a very significant impact, both positive and negative, on the way people view us. We are particularly vulnerable when people know us to supposedly be Christians. People will judge us by the way we behave.

Now back to my specific problem. I don't want to be guilty of putting other people off Christianity because of the way I behave—because I can't keep control of what I say or because I talk about other people behind their backs. I think that sometimes some of us feel that it's okay to say negative things about other people if someone else starts bad-mouthing them first. But it's not OK. I should not feel that that is a reason to do the same. I have to resist that temptation. Also, I have to make sure that this is not becoming a habit or a trap into which I fall.

We each have our personal mission to spread Christ's message of love and kindness to our fellow man. We don't give a positive image for Christianity, or for ourselves, if we are the type of people who say unkind things to or about others. People will know we are Christians by our love—by our care and concern for others.

So I keep telling myself, "If I haven't got anything good to say about someone, then I shouldn't bother saying anything at all."

Travel Tip to Remember
Remember you are always on duty as a Christian. You are being noticed, whether consciously or unconsciously, by those around you. If your words and actions are held in evidence against you, how will you fare?

Luke 6:42

How can you say to your brother, 'Brother, let me remove that splinter in your eye,' when you do not even notice the wooden beam in your own eye? You hypocrite! Remove the wooden beam from your eye first; then you will see clearly to remove the splinter in your brother's eye.

Chapter

36

I want to discuss my hair, and, specifically, the hair on the back of my head. Apparently, I have a bit of a bald spot there. Of course, I have never seen it directly. I can't see it unless I take the trouble to get a mirror and position it in such a way that I can see the back of my head.

The back of the head always seems to have been a problem for me. I remember that, as a child, every morning I would go into my mom and dad's room to brush my hair, and nearly every morning when I thought that I had finished brushing my hair, my Dad would say, "Peter, you have got to remember that you have a back to your head. Brush the back of your head because your hair is still sticking up."

Isn't that true in life? We carry on doing the same things day after day. We comb the hair or correct the things that we can see, the things that are obvious, the things that are apparent, yet we infrequently step back and take a mirror to ourselves to take a closer look at the things that perhaps others see but we don't.

And that's one of the clear exhortations Christ makes in the New Testament. Don't spend your time looking at how others can be improved. Rather, take a good look at yourself. The scripture passage about the beam in the eye is one of the better known. However, I would like to take a look at it in a slightly different way.

Let me explain.

In my early life, while I was studying law in England, I had the privilege of interviewing many prisoners in jail awaiting trial or appeal. I met with murderers, armed robbers, and people who had committed heinous crimes. The one thing that I consistently found was that, if I took the trouble to really listen, to let them talk and then conversed with them, each and every one of them had intrinsic goodness in them.

It may have been well hidden, but it was definitely there, and it started to come through the more I let them talk and the more I was open to properly listening to them and discussing with them.

Very often, people seem to display a false exterior, or perhaps a better description is a false image: an image of the "false self" that hides the "true self" inside that person. We all have goodness in us. That is our true self. It's just that sometimes the true self, the good self, the real self, is prevented from coming out by the false self that we have created around our persona. This is because people are so often the products of their environment. This not only applies to criminals; it also applies to many of us from all walks of life. We have created an image of ourselves from which it is sometimes difficult to get away.

I believe that it is our individual responsibility to try to discover that true self that is within each of us and have the courage to let that true self, the goodness that is within each and every one of us, shine through.

What I am suggesting is that in seeking to remove the beam from our own eye, as Jesus exhorts us, we do so not so much by just looking for our faults but more by looking for the basic goodness inherent in each of us and letting it come through. Therefore, by looking for and removing those false personas that are perhaps preventing that full goodness from coming out, then maybe we won't even notice the splinters in other people's eyes, or, perhaps with kindness in our hearts, we will see through the so-called imperfections in others and focus directly on their intrinsic goodness.

Travel Tip to Remember
Step back. Take a look at yourself spiritually. Let your goodness: your "true self" shine through. See if there are problems or obstacles holding you back from being one with God. This will also improve your ability to see and more fully appreciate the goodness in others that is so often blinded to us.

Peter J. Moriarty

Acts: 4:10-16

...let it be known and clearly understood by all of you, and by all the people of Israel, that in the name of Jesus Christ the Nazarene, whom you [demanded be] crucified [by the Romans and], whom God raised from the dead—in this name [that is, by the authority and power of Jesus] this man stands here before you in good health. This Jesus is "the stone which was despised and rejected by you, the builders but which became the chief cornerstone." And there is salvation in no one else; for there is no other name under heaven that has been given among people by which we must be saved [for God has provided the world no alternative for salvation].

Now when the men of the Sanhedrin (Jewish High Court) saw the confidence and boldness of Peter and John, and grasped the fact that they were uneducated and untrained [ordinary] men, they were astounded, and began to recognize that they had been with Jesus. And seeing the man who had been healed standing there with them, they had nothing to say in reply. But after ordering them to step out of the Council [chamber], they began to confer among themselves, saying, "What are we to do with these men? For the fact that an extraordinary miracle has taken place through them is public knowledge and clearly evident to all the residents of Jerusalem, and we cannot deny it."

Chapter

37

Have you ever stood up and spoken in public to a group of people about your religious beliefs? If you have, I am sure you have experienced people praising you for helping to bring others closer to God.

That is great, so long as we keep everything in proportion—so long as we know what part we played and what part God played. We must always be careful not to stray into the realm of the dangerous sin of pride.

In these situations, we have to be thankful for having been given the opportunity to speak out publicly about the kingdom of God while always being mindful that it is God, not you or me, who should be thanked and praised. It is too easy for most of us to wallow in praise, thinking that we are the "be all and end all" of everything—that things have been achieved because we are "so great."

Likewise, when people say that they would never feel comfortable speaking in public, and particularly about their religious beliefs, they need to be reminded of the story in the gospel where it stated, "Observing the boldness of Peter and John and perceiving them to be uneducated, ordinary men, they were amazed."

I truly believe that we are all called to go beyond our comfort zone. Even if we believe that we are "uneducated, ordinary men" as Peter and John were referred to, we are called to love every human being. That "call to love" means that we have an obligation to reach out to our fellow man, particularly the ones who have drifted away from Christianity and those who have never known Christianity.

We all have responsibility to spread the Gospel, and we all have responsibility to each other. We are the Church, the body of Christ on earth. Christ said that "when two or three are gathered together in my name there I am in the midst of them." The community is the church. Church is not the bricks and mortar. It is the community that makes up the church. Whether we accept it or not, we all need community. To illustrate this, I want to refer to a story told by one of our priests during a sermon. He told the story of a man who had stopped going to church but remained friends with the pastor. Periodically, the pastor would go to the man's house, and on one occasion, as they sat by a blazing log fire, the pastor leaned forward and, with the help of a poker, pulled out a burning log from all the rest of the burning logs. The two men sat in silence as the isolated log gradually lost all of its fire and warmth and died out while the rest of the logs in the fireplace burned vigorously together. Looking at it, the man said to the pastor, "I see your point. I'll come back to church."

He realized that he needed the fire and the nourishment of the community: the church.

Travel Tip to Remember
Be prepared and committed to go beyond your comfort zone in spreading the Good News of our salvation. The first step is always the hardest. It gets easier thereafter. Have total confidence that God will always be there to help you.

"WAY to go!"

Luke 10:25-28

There was a scholar of the law who stood up to test him and said, "Teacher, what must I do to inherit eternal life?" Jesus said to him, "What is written in the law? How do you read it?" He said in reply, "You shall love the Lord, your God, with all your heart, with all your being, with all your strength, and with all your mind, and your neighbor as yourself." He replied to him, "You have answered correctly; do this and you will live."

Chapter

38

A few years ago, I was in another country over the Fourth of July weekend. While I was there, I experienced an amusing incident that I thought was so reflective of life in general, and specifically my own spiritual life.

I was at the fish market trying to buy three pounds of shrimp. I had just agreed to the price per pound with the fishmonger, after which he went to weigh the shrimp on some mechanical scales. Seeing this, I insisted that the shrimp be weighed on his electronic scales. I did this because on past visits to this store, the fishmonger had told me that the reason that prices were lower at the other stores was because they were cheating by using mechanical scales instead of using accurate electronic scales.

When I insisted that he use the electronic scales, he tried to tell me at first that they were not working properly. Despite my protests, he proceeded to weigh out three pounds on the mechanical scales. I continued to complain and eventually he gave in and put the supposed three pounds of shrimp onto the electronic scale. Immediately, the scale registered the shrimp as weighing less than two pounds. At this point, the fishmonger protested that, "You cannot have the price I quoted and accurate scales!"

I burst out laughing. It took the heat out of the situation, but I certainly did not buy the shrimp from him.

I think that this is similar to the way that I am sometimes with God. Perhaps many of us are. We try to get away with giving God as little as possible but expect God to treat us fairly. We sometimes do just enough to make us feel good but not enough to make a full commitment to God. We will give two pounds, but we are not going to give God the three proper pounds that he wants from us.

I think that sometimes as Christians living in today's world, we are almost allowed to get away with doing the bare minimum. But doing the bare minimum is just not enough. We are the followers of Jesus Christ. We are his disciples and, by our baptism, we are charged with spreading the Good News, rescuing the lost, and leading others to the Father through His son, Jesus, the Christ. It's not easy work. It requires our full "three pounds" of commitment.

Ask yourself, "Am I a two or three pounds of shrimp type of Christian?"

Travel Tip to Remember
Don't try to get away with doing as little as possible in your pursuit of Christianity and in leading people to Jesus. The path to heaven requires us to be a "three pounds of shrimp" type of Christian.

"WAY to go!"

Matthew 6:19-21

*Do not store up for yourselves treasures on earth, where
moth and decay destroy, and thieves break in and
steal. But store up treasures in heaven, where neither moth
nor decay destroys, nor thieves break in and steal. For
where your treasure is, there also will your heart be.*

Philippians 3:14

*I continue my pursuit toward the goal, the prize of God's
upward calling, in Christ Jesus.*

Chapter

39

I had just turned 30 when I walked out into Kenya's Amboseli Game Park. It was early morning, and I looked across the vast plain, where I saw elephant, giraffes, and Thomson's gazelles feeding, and there, looming tall on the horizon, stood Mount Kilimanjaro in all of its magnificence.

I stood in awe, wonder, and pride. Yes pride. I was proud that I had achieved my goal of being able to live and work overseas, and particularly in being able to live in such an exciting and beautiful country.

As stated earlier in this book, as a young adult I was extremely ambitious: a go getter—someone who would literally go to the ends of earth to achieve the career goals that I had set for myself. And that is literally what I had to do.

My wife and I had had three children before we were 28 years of age. Clearly, we had a lot of responsibilities as parents at a fairly young age but, for my part, I also craved responsibility in my career. I knew that, if I was going to get the career responsibilities that I wanted and the commensurate level of salary that would enable me to support my family, I had to find an extraordinary position. At that time, England had been going through very tough economic times, and I had come to the conclusion that, in order to achieve my goals, I would have no choice but to try to find an overseas position. I had realized that, at my age in England, it was probably not going to be possible for me to get the level of responsibility and the sort of financial compensation I desired.

Shortly after the birth of our third child, I clearly realized that I did not have the experience necessary to get the type of job I really wanted, despite trying very hard and applying for many such positions. I, therefore, decided to take a move in my company that would provide me with the international experience I thought I needed.

When I was 29 years of age, I was approached by an executive recruiter concerning an overseas position. However, the interviews for that position were arduous and literally took me to the ends of the earth. I was interviewed first in London, England. The second set of interviews was held in Lucerne, Switzerland. The third set in Hong Kong, and the fourth interview was in Nairobi, Kenya. After being interviewed in Nairobi, I had to fly for a final set of interviews in Athens, Greece. After that, I was offered a contract as an expatriate manager based in that company's Nairobi office, with responsibility for eight East African countries. As a consequence, just as I reached the age of 30, I arrived in Kenya with my wife and three young children. This would be our home for the next few years.

I think that many people can relate to the goal setting, ambition, determination, and drive that are part and parcel of striving for a successful career. But how many of us apply the same level effort and determination to the achievement of spiritual goals? How many people actually have defined spiritual goals and a time frame within which each goal is to be achieved?

It's all too easy to leave spiritual goal setting until another day or even a later part of our lives. The reality is that spiritual goal setting might take many of us out of our comfort zone, and that is understandable. The real challenge is taking the first step, and to quote Lao Tzu, "The journey of a thousand miles begins with one step."

It is important—if we want to be successful in making our journey along the path to eternal life—that we define the spiritual goals we need to achieve and the time frames within which we aim to achieve each of those goals. Don't leave it to another day. Take that first step and enjoy the journey.

Remember that your journey will be so much more enjoyable if you learn to fully appreciate all of the many blessings that are often just taken for granted by most of us. Appreciate the blessings of family and friends. Appreciate the beauty of everything around you: the sunshine, the flowers, and the many other little wonders of the world.

These are blessings that enable us to see our ultimate spiritual goal of being one with God. These are the blessings that enable us to see God in every created thing.

Travel tip to Remember
Don't just focus on career or worldly goals or even bucket lists. Prepare yourself a set of spiritual goals and time frames in which to achieve each of those goals as you travel along your path towards achieving eternal life. Remember that every journey begins with the first step.

Peter J. Moriarty

Take that first step and enjoy the views of God's marvelous creation along the way.

"WAY to go!"

Peter J. Moriarty

Matthew 4:18-22

As he was walking by the Sea of Galilee, he saw two brothers, Simon who is called Peter, and his brother Andrew, casting a net into the sea; they were fishermen. He said to them, "Come after me, and I will make you fishers of men." At once they left their nets and followed him. He walked along from there and saw two other brothers, James, the son of Zebedee, and his brother John. They were in a boat, with their father Zebedee, mending their nets. He called them, and immediately they left their boat and their father and followed him.

Chapter

40

I often think that we may have made our practice of religion too complicated. It was, after all, designed to be taught to, and be understood by, the uneducated as well as the educated. Christ seems to have pitched it, as it were, at the lowest common denominator.

I think that Christ might be very disappointed by what we have done with Christianity. We have made it so complex that the ordinary man and woman in the street cannot grasp some of the doctrines and theological concepts that the Church bands around. As a result, the ordinary man in the street often ends up blindly following or even rejecting Christianity instead of embracing the teachings of Christ and making those teachings a part of his or her life. In many instances, our religious practices may seem in complete contradiction to Christ's words: "For my yolk is easy and my burden is light."

It could be argued that this complexity has resulted in one of the biggest travesties since the foundation of Christianity, namely the divisions that exist among the Christian denominations. Most, if not all, of the reasons for the divisions, are not understood by the vast majority of followers of Christ. These divisions could have been avoided and should now be put behind us to bring about the unity of all Christians. Christianity would then be a far more powerful force in the world.

Just look who Jesus chose for his executive team. He walked along the shore of the Sea of Galilee, and he chose Simon and his brother Andrew, a couple of lowly fishermen. He then spotted two more fishermen mending their nets, namely James and John. He asked all four of these fishermen to follow him. Follow him where? In the next part of the gospel, we read of this group arriving in the town of Capernaum. It might be true to say that the average citizen of Capernaum might have been forgiven for thinking that this was a most unlikely group: a band of fishermen led by a carpenter from some "out of the way" town called Nazareth. At one point in the gospel, the following is commented: "Can anything good come from Nazareth?"

Furthermore, later in the gospel, we read that, on the Sabbath, the leader of this unlikely group went into the synagogue and started teaching. We read that he taught with authority and the people were astonished. Whoever would have believed it? This carpenter from Nazareth really knew his stuff and spoke almost with the voice of God.

If Jesus wanted to show us how to lead our lives, how to love the Father and our fellow man, by giving us absolutely complex doctrines, he would not have chosen the team that he did. He almost certainly would not have chosen uneducated fishermen as his core team to spread the word and take it to the nations. He would not have spent so much time showing his love and understanding for the poorest of the poor, for those who had fallen off the edges of society, if what he wanted to impart to them was complicated and beyond their level of understanding. He would have made sure that his focus was on the well-educated members of society. Yet he did not do that. Jesus gave us a simple message of how we should lead our lives with love of God and love for our fellow man. If we focus on these the greatest commandments and we truly take them to heart and lead our lives following those commandments, we will not go wrong. We have to love God with our whole heart, our whole soul, and our whole mind, and love our neighbor as ourselves. In other words, we have to be selfless in the way we treat our fellow man. It's as simple as that.

Jesus was a great teacher. He astonished the people with the simplicity of his message. It was a message that everyone could understand and could apply to their lives. In its simplicity, however, the teachings of Jesus were and are challenging. They are challenging because mankind is intrinsically selfish, and Christ's teachings are all about being selfless. This is the simple truth, and Jesus taught us to focus on overcoming that selfishness in order to prepare us to be with him in the Kingdom of Heaven.

In the gospel of Matthew (25:34-36), Christ gave us clear and unambiguous guidelines of what we need to do if we want to ensure that we successfully reach our Heavenly destination when he said,

"Come, you who are blessed by my Father. Inherit the kingdom prepared for you from the foundation of the world. For I was hungry and you gave me food, I was thirsty and you gave me drink, a stranger and you welcomed me, naked and you clothed me, ill and you cared for me, in prison and you visited me."

It's as simple as that. That's the "WAY to go."

Travel Tip to Remember

Don't make your practice of religion overly complicated or burdensome. Remember that Jesus chose simple people with little education to be the ones to educate the rest of the world. Focus on the imperatives of Christianity (and humanity) in order to ensure that you successfully navigate the path to Heaven. Love God with your whole heart, soul, and being, and demonstrate your love for God and your fellow man by feeding the hungry, providing refreshment to those that thirst, welcoming strangers and those on the margins of society, by clothing and sheltering those without means, and by being present and providing comfort to those who find themselves in difficult circumstances.

"WAY to go!"

Peter J. Moriarty

Summary

We have to be very careful not to let the practice of our religion or adherence to man-made religious rules become a substitution for or a distraction from us performing good deeds and consistently leading our lives the way our Father requires of us, as revealed through the teachings of His son, Jesus, the Christ. The WAY to Heaven is not hard. Remember the words of Jesus when he said in Matthew 11:30:

"My yoke is easy and my burden is light."

The WAY bears repeating. It just requires us to:

- Feed the hungry
- Give drink to the thirsty
- Welcome the stranger
- Clothe the naked and those in need
- Take care of the sick
- Visit and provide comfort to those in prison and in any sort of distress.

This is the "WAY to go!"

Peter J. Moriarty

Acknowledgements

I want to acknowledge and thank my wife, Elizabeth, and my friend, Alan Mulhern, both of whom provided me with encouragement, critical feedback, and valuable suggestions as I labored to finalize the manuscript.

I also want to thank Nick May for editing the manuscript and for his willingness to always go the extra mile to assist me.

Additionally, I want to acknowledge and thank Alonzo Butler, of Butler Designs, New Orleans, for the graphic design and layout of the cover.

References

All scriptural references have been taken from the New American Bible (Revised Edition).

Peter J. Moriarty

About the Author

Peter Moriarty is a British-born American citizen living in Scottsdale, Arizona. He has spent the majority of his life in the healthcare industry, originally as a pharmaceutical industry executive where he had the opportunity to live in a number of different countries, and subsequently as an entrepreneur, having founded a number of business ventures. Peter was a co-founder of Shire Pharmaceuticals, a highly successful company now employing many thousands of employees all over the world. However, he is quick to point-out that not all of his entrepreneurial ventures have been successful. Some have been money-draining failures. He has learned to face and deal with adversity as well as good fortune, and he doesn't give-up. He has tremendous support from his family and an enduring faith in God and the teachings of Jesus Christ. While Peter is still active in another pharmaceutical company that he co-founded, he is also the owner of The Goals Institute, a 25-year-old training and development company. This provides him with the opportunity to pursue his passion for conducting training seminars, undertaking public speaking engagements, and also coaching executives on a one-on-one basis.

Peter J. Moriarty

The Goals Institute

For more information about The Goals Institute visit

www.goalsinstitute.com

or contact

info@goalsinstitute.com

Made in the USA
San Bernardino, CA
02 March 2019